COLLECTED W.

THE CROSS OF CHRIST

PLUS BONUS MINI BOOK:

UPSIDE-DOWN VALUES: THE BEATITUDES

COMPILED BY HAYES PRESS

Published by:

HAYES PRESS

The Barn, Flaxlands

Royal Wootton Bassett

Swindon, SN4 8DY

United Kingdom

www.hayespress.org

CHAPTER ONE: CURSED ON THE TREE (IAN PENN)

The Tree

Xylophones occur in every country. They are most simply made of pieces of wood which are cut to different lengths so that each emits a different musical note when struck with a wooden hammer. They get their name from the Greek words for a piece of wood, xulon, and of course, phone, meaning sound. As some may know, those who study plants, botanists, have chosen this word to describe technically woody material; they call it xylem.

The word is found in the New Testament where it refers to the sawn-off pieces of wood, the staves, with which those who came to arrest the Lord Jesus were armed (Matt.26:47,55; Mk.14:43,48; Lk.22:52). Similarly, the word is used of the stocks which imprisoned Paul and Silas (Acts 16:24) and were clearly man-made pieces of wood deliberately cut and shaped for that purpose. It is used also to describe the wood used in buildings (1 Cor.3:12) and carved into vessels (Rev.18:12).

Thus, it is a word that is not used to describe a naturally occurring, living, growing tree, but rather refers to a piece of tree, deliberately cut and fashioned for a man-made purpose. This too is the word for the dead, dry wood, the tree ready for destruction of which the Lord Himself spoke (Lk.23:31). In what He said, He may have been hinting at what was to befall Himself for this is the very word used of the tree on which He was hanged and accursed (Gal.3:13). He was hanged upon a man-made wooden spike, a piece of wood deliberately cut and fashioned for its awful purpose; to display a man put to a felon's death.

The Cross

At first sight, 'the tree' is an expression as fearfully evocative as modern phrases such as 'the stake', meaning the place of execution by fire or 'the gibbet' meaning the place of execution by hanging, or 'the block' meaning the place of execution by beheading. Another word, 'the cross', more accurately corresponds to these expressions. 'The cross' is the word which refers to the place and manner of execution of the Lord Jesus Christ. It depicts death by torture, death in a particularly humiliating fashion; so much so that 'the death of the cross' is the lowest level to which the Lord humbled Himself (Phil.2:8). It was a death associated with deepest shame (Heb.12:2), but shame inflicted by men.

The man-made origin of the humiliation is well seen in the Lord's metaphorical references to the Cross to describe the spectacle to which men may put the faithful disciple who must 'take up his cross' (Matt.10:38; Matt.16:24; Mk.8:34; Lk.9:23) and 'bear his own cross' (Lk.14:27). The faithful disciple will find himself in the place of rejection because he rejects worldly standards and values. He is prepared to lose his life completely in his Lord's service. In so doing he follows his Lord, and just as the Lord looked beyond the humiliation to the joy that followed (Heb.12:2) so the disciple may look with joy to his day of reward (Matt.5:11,12).

The Curse

Hanging on a tree was not a form of execution decreed by the Law of Moses. It was a practice reserved for crimes deemed so bad that a spectacle was to be made, not of the felon's execution, but of his body in death (Deut.21:22,23). It was in the first place a demonstration to all of what society thought of his crime. But the society concerned was that of the people of God who worshipped in the house of God, and the Law that was broken was not man's law but the Law of God. In the second place, the disapproval was not only man's but God's. Hanging the body on the tree demonstrated not merely exceptional disapproval by God but subjection to the curse of God. So serious was the divine judgement that the body was not to stay where it was a moment longer than the light of the day on which the deed was done.

Were it to hang a moment longer, the very ground of the holy land itself would be defiled. Thus, hanging on the tree represented something far worse than the death of the cross. The cross showed man wreaking his cruelty on the living criminal, but the tree demonstrated the very wrath of God.

The Crime

Although the highest Council of Israel in the Lord's day was determined to put Him to death, His accusers needed to get the approval of the Roman authorities. It is not clear that when they brought the Lord to Pilate to seek the death penalty they knew He would be crucified. There is no doubt, however, that they did know when Pilate sought to release Him because, when Pilate sought to leave the decision about the death penalty to the Jewish people, their rulers whipped up the crowd to demand crucifixion.

They knew it was the inevitable penalty when it became clear that Pilate was offering Christ as a substitute for the convicted murderer, Barabbas. There was worse to come, however, because they went to Pilate to hasten the deaths of the executed men to ensure they would not remain hanging at eventide, when the Sabbath began (Jn.19:31). Their act shows that they clearly knew that they were carrying out the Law of the Lord (Deut.21:22,23).

Thus they knew equally that by hanging their enemy on the Cross they were hanging Him on the Tree and deliberately bringing Him under the worst condemnation possible, the curse of God.

The Charge

In Jerusalem at the start of the new dispensation, Peter repeatedly laid the crucifixion of Christ at the door of the Jews and their leaders (Acts 2:23,36; Acts 3:12-15; Acts 4:10). The leaders were impressed and somewhat afraid at the spread of the message which, in spite of their efforts to suppress it, had filled Jerusalem. Their outrage at the very idea that they might be at fault shows that they still thought they were in the right. Appearing before the very Council that had condemned the Lord, Peter mentioned the Tree (Acts 5:30), linking with it the need for the repentance of Israel, their Israel, and their hearts were cut. These were men who knew the significance of being hanged on a tree.

The teaching of the Apostles had filled Jerusalem. An unlettered man who, a few weeks before had been so weak outside their chambers, was denouncing them to their face. Such success must show that God was with the Apostles and not with the Council. If so, the Council's decision must have been wrong and it must be the Council who deserved the curse of God. Alas, though they were convicted they were not converted, and determined like Pharaoh of old, to preserve their own position whatever the rights and wrongs of the matter.

The charge was repeated when the gospel was taken to the Gentiles (Acts 10:39). Cornelius and his companions were familiar with Jewish custom and practice, but in their case the message of the Tree was not restricted to Jewish responsibility alone. The One who became a curse was proclaimed as Judge of all, the living and the dead, whether Jew or Gentile. Similarly, the accompanying message of forgiveness of sins was to everyone, Jew and Gentile, who believed on Him. So the message of the Tree had in it something which spoke to Gentile hearts.

The sequence recurred in a Gentile land, initially amongst well-taught Jews in the synagogue of Antioch of Pisidia (Acts 13:14-52). Here again, the Jewish leaders' determination to slay an innocent man and the message of the Tree lay at the heart of Paul's account (Acts 13:28,29). In this case it was connected again with forgiveness of sins, but also with justification for everyone (Jews and Gentiles) who believed (Acts 13:48,49). What was it about the message of the Tree that reached those who were not directly implicated in ensuring that the death of Christ was such that He came under the curse of God?

The Crux

The decisive point at issue in the message of the Tree is given in the epistles by Peter and Paul, the two who spoke about it in the Acts (see Gal.3:10-14 and 1 Pet.2:23,24). By their actions, the leaders of the Jews brought a wholly innocent, indeed perfect, Man under the curse of God. They broke their own Law and so, breaking the Law in one part, became guilty of all. So the Law became a curse to all under it because, breaking it in many parts, they became guilty of all and under its condemnation. The principle extends to all men, since all are subject to divine Law (Rom.2:14-16; Gal.3:11). Since Christ bore all men's sins when He endured the wrath of God on the Tree (1 Pet.2:24), so all men have played their part in His death on the Tree, just as surely as did the Jews and their Leaders at the time.

Similarly, just as forgiveness was preached to those directly implicated in bringing Christ under the curse of God, so it is also preached to all those who, by their sins for which they are condemned, caused Him to suffer as their Substitute.

The Christian Curriculum of the Tree

When taken in sequence, the five New Testament scriptures which elaborate the ordinance of the Law concerning the Tree (Deut.21:22,23) focus on Christ, get to the crux of the gospel, and tell us something of the heart of God. As to the gospel, they begin with the need for personal conviction on behalf of each person who is implicated in the wrath of God falling upon Christ. Conviction is to be followed by repentance which leads to forgiveness (Acts 5:30,31). To this is added the alternative of Christ as Judge or as the One in whom faith is to be placed for salvation (Acts 10:39-43) resulting in justification by faith (Acts 13:29,30).

Finally, the basis of such salvation is shown to lie in His death on the Tree as the sinner's substitute (Gal.3:10-14), enduring the curse of God for the sinner's actual sins (1 Pet.2:24). 'Cursed ... on the Tree' tells us, too, of the lovingkindness of the heart of God. Every scripture which speaks of Christ on the Tree, whether spoken by Peter or Paul, men who knew the Law of Moses intimately, is directed firstly at men and women who had a like knowledge. Each, too, is followed immediately by a reference to Christ's exaltation and to the blessings of salvation which flow from His death on the Tree:

> "The God of our fathers raised up Jesus, whom ye slew, hanging him on a tree. Him did God exalt with his right hand to be a Prince and a Saviour, for to give repentance to Israel, and remission of sins" (Acts 5:30,31).

"And we are witnesses of all things which he did both in the country of the Jews, and in Jerusalem; whom also they slew, hanging him on a tree. Him God raised up the third day, and gave him to be made manifest ..." (Acts 10:39,40).

"And when they had fulfilled all things that were written of him, they took him down from the tree, and laid him in a tomb. But God raised him from the dead" (Acts 13:29,30).

"Christ redeemed us from the curse of the law, having become a curse for us: for it is written, Cursed is every one that hangeth on a tree: that upon the Gentiles might come the blessing of Abraham in Christ Jesus (Gal.3:13,14).

"Who his own self bare our sins in his body upon the tree, that we, having died unto sins, might live unto righteousness; by whose stripes ye were healed" (1 Pet.2:24).

It is as though God would have even the most instructed to know that the ignominy which befell His beloved Son has so affected His heart that He wishes men and women not to linger on it without considering the glory which surpasses it.

CHAPTER TWO: STANDING BY THE CROSS (KEITH DORRICOTT)

Some sat at Calvary, their work done; some watched as they passed by; some stood and watched. They divided themselves by reaction, just as old Simeon had prophesied at Jesus' birth: "... this Child is destined for the fall and rising of many in Israel, and for a sign which will be spoken against ... that the thoughts of many hearts may be revealed" (1). Calvary's few hours revealed those thoughts.

Those Who Sat

Crucifixion had been carried out by four Roman soldiers under a centurion. Neither their deeds nor their victims would have appeared remarkable. Then they sat guarding One whom the crowd was challenging to save Himself. None tried to rescue Him. A King without a kingdom in spite of Pilate's inscription. They jeered too, and offered Him sour vinegar wine as a sedative. He refused it, not answering their shouts nor showing hatred. They had heard Him ask His God, 'Father, forgive them, for they know not what they do' (2). What kind of man would pray for them while they were so spitefully abusing Him (3)?

But at noon when the sun should have been its brightest, intense darkness blotted out a view of the crosses at even a few feet. No motion, no sound now. No pretence at guarding the Prisoner now. They waited for three long hours. Then, as light returned, Jesus shouted out in Hebrew. Then He called out, 'I thirst' (4). Seemingly His first concession to pain and weakness. This time He took the cheap wine offered to Him on a sponge.

Very quickly the sky cleared and Jesus cried loudly, 'It is finished!' (5) then, 'Father, into Your hands I commit my Spirit' (6). He was dead! Crucified people did not die that quickly, and especially after a shout like that. And then the ground started to rumble. An earth-quake! People scrambled to safety as the rocks broke around them. The soldiers could see that their centurion was also in awe. He knew he had just executed an innocent man. And Jesus with full dignity and determination had entered death. Their declaration showed their thought: 'Truly this was the Son of God!' (7).

Those Who Passed By

The Place of the Skull was very close to the city - just close to a busy road that Passover weekend. The arrest, trial and crucifixion had been accomplished in record time (about twelve hours). Jewish leaders had done an effective propaganda job. Many in the crowd believed He was an imposter, a blasphemer, a dangerous political radical. It was important to dispose of Him quickly. And so there were many residents and visitors to Jerusalem who saw Him hanging there as they walked past. And His accusation was in three languages, to make sure everyone knew. They had heard of Him all right, but it seemed so incongruous.

Previously, wherever this man went, a crowd had followed Him. His reputation was that He frequently healed people miraculously, even raised some that were dead. He had sounded invincible. But now they were seeing the real Jesus for themselves. He did not have miraculous powers, or else He would not still be on that Cross. How could someone who could bring back a person from death not save Himself? And so they shook their heads and shouted out at Him, without even stopping in their tracks, reminding Him of what they had (erroneously) heard that He had claimed: to be able to destroy and rebuild Herod's Temple in three days (8). That was the height of self-delusion.

And so they blasphemed Him, repeating those cynical words that the Devil himself had used in the wilderness three years before: 'If you are the Son of God ...' (9). And so, as they kept walking away from the Cross, they would not believe in such a self-deluded imposter. Three days later, unknown to them wherever they were by then, there took place the ultimate attestation of the validity of the claims of Christ as to His identity. He did not make it Himself. It was not His disciples who made it. But it was enough to silence these and all men, and silence Satan himself. It was made by God the Father 'according to the working of His mighty power which He worked in Christ when He raised Him from the dead' (10). How sad it was for those passers-by whose hearts were so full of rejection and ridicule, that they did not pause on their journey, to stop and watch more closely. Where were they going that was more important than this?

Those Who Stood and Watched

(a) The leaders and the people

Most prominent among the observers were those leaders of the Jews who stayed to see the completion of their plan. They had objected to Pilate's superscription on Jesus' Cross, but had been overruled. What a weight of responsibility was on these men! Under the Law, when they sinned, they brought guilt on the people (11). Perhaps they had recognized this when the people had cried out at His trial, 'His blood be on us and on our children' (12), although they disputed responsibility later (13). They knew and taught the Old Testament scriptures. They, more than anyone, should have recognized Jesus and welcomed Him as the long-awaited Messiah from God. Greater knowledge brings greater responsibility, which is why the Lord had said that such a person had greater sin than Pilate did. But even Pilate recognized what was driving them – they were envious of Him

(14) - and their envy was clouding their judgement and their understanding.

No fewer than eight Old Testament scriptures were specifically fulfilled during the six hours that Christ was on the Cross, in addition to the many prior to this. They should have known. They even quoted one themselves, from Psalm 22, without realizing that two other portions of the very same Psalm were also being fulfilled before their eyes (15). When Jesus called out to His God: 'Eli, Eli ...' (16) they failed to recognize the words of Psalm 22 but thought He was appealing to Elias (Elijah). But it was to Elijah not many days before that He had spoken on the Mount of Transfiguration about His decease, which He was about to accomplish in Jerusalem (17). This they did not understand. They had the arrogance of ignorance.

Even the supernatural events of the day had little apparent effect. But they certainly affected the crowd, who had been watching from a distance. They saw the way Christ approached death, observed His silence towards His accusers, and heard His loud cry at the end. They saw and felt the darkness and the earthquake; and they saw how He expired. When they saw it all, they beat their breasts in horror, and turned away. But what would move the hearts of those leaders? Their concern was merely to get the bodies down from the crosses so not to defile the land on the Sabbath day (18). What would they think when they saw what had happened to the veil protecting the inner sanctuary of their temple? But perhaps, silently, some of them may have begun to be affected by what they saw that day. Because later, as the apostles preached the gospel of the resurrected Christ around Jerusalem, we read that: "a great many of the priests were obedient to the faith" (19).

(b) The disciples

But there was one group of people about which we read surprisingly little concerning Calvary. Where were His eleven apostles? We know John was there, but where were the others? Were they included with 'His acquaintances' (20) who were standing afar off? Or were they too afraid even to be there, unless they too should be implicated? They had scattered from Him at Gethsemane when He had been arrested. They had not supported

Him in His agony there; were they missing here also? They were to be 'the little flock' to whom the Father was going to give the kingdom (21). They were to be the ones to carry on Jesus' work after His departure. But where were they now? "Strike the Shepherd, and the sheep will be scattered", the scripture had said (22), and this too must be fulfilled. It would take the resurrection of Christ, that great Shepherd of the sheep, with the blood of the everlasting covenant, to unite them again (23). They would be joined to Him and to each other under the new covenant.

(c) The women

But, not surprisingly, there was one small group of disciples who are mentioned quite specifically at Calvary. Many of their names are given. They were the women, not frequently mentioned, but always there from Galilee to Judea to care for Him. There was no doubting what was in their hearts. 'Now there stood by the cross of Jesus His mother' (24). Where else would she be? Others were afar off, but she was close by. To others He was the great Messiah; to her He was also her son. What was in her heart as she watched Him suffering there? Was she thinking back over all the things she had pondered from His birth - the words of the angel, of Elizabeth, of the shepherds, of Simeon, of Anna? Surely at this moment she would be remembering Simeon's words: "yes, a sword will pierce through your own soul also" (25).

And then Jesus saw her, and John standing nearby. She needed a son to love; she needed a son to care for her. And, despite His all-absorbing agony, He said to her: "Woman, behold your son!" and to John: "Behold your mother!" (26). Perhaps no one else heard it, but for Mary it provided comfort for a stricken heart. What about our hearts today? As you and I are drawn again to the details of the events of that unique day, the thoughts of our hearts too are revealed. Had we been there, which group would we have been in? Would we have been blinded by ignorance, fear or envy? Or would we have been in awe of who was on that Cross and what He was accomplishing there for us, and would our hearts also have been drawn out to exclaim: "Truly this is the Son of God?"

Teach me

"Teach me your way, O LORD; lead me in a straight path" (Ps.27:11).

"Show me your ways, O LORD, teach me your paths; guide me in your truth and teach me" (Ps.25:4,5).

"Teach me, and I will be quiet; show me where I have been wrong" (Job 6:24).

Biblical references (all from the NKJV): (1) Lk.2:34,35 (2) Lk.23:34 (3) Matt.5:44 (4) Jn.19:28 (5) Jn.19:30 (6) Lk.23:46 (7) Matt.27:54 (8) Jn.2:19 (9) Matt.27:40; Lk.4:3 (10) Eph.1:19,20 (11) Lev.4:3 (12) Matt.27:25 (13) Acts 5:28 (14) Matt.27:18 (15) Ps.22:8,1,18 (16) Matt.27:46 (17) Lk.9:30,31 (18) Deut.21:23 (19) Acts 6:7 (20) Lk.23:49 (21) Lk.12:32 (22) Zech.13:7 (23) Heb.13:20 (24) Jn.19:25 (25) Lk.2:35-36; Jn.19:26,27

CHAPTER THREE: THE BLOOD OF HIS CROSS (ALAN SANDS)

You might have heard of *The Red River of Life,* a fascinating Christian-produced documentary depicting the marvels of our blood circulatory system. Such a production engenders a real sense of awe at the Creator's handiwork in our bloodstream - the constant vital flow of the great mystery of life itself. This chapter concerns an even more awe-inspiring theme – the shed blood of Christ and the greater mysteries of eternal life which flow therefrom. As Charles Wesley puts it: *Pardon and life flowed from His side, When He our Lord was crucified.* No contemplation of the crosswork of Christ, with its unparalleled sufferings for Him, its profound consequences for creation, and its wealth of spiritual blessings for ourselves, should ever leave us unmoved, and hopefully our present theme will be no exception.

The phrase 'the blood of His cross' is from Colossians 1:20, and reference will be made to its context later. Meanwhile, we recall our Lord's momentous pronouncement on the eve of the crucifixion, "My blood of the new covenant ... is shed for many for the remission of sins" (Matt.26:28). Yes, it's His blood *shed* which has achieved so much and that is now the subject before us. The sight of blood often means that something is wrong and it can even fill us with great horror. But the paradox is that through divine intervention such a gory sight has become the source of the greatest hope! The obvious example is the deliverance from slavery and death enshrined in God's promise, "When I see the blood, I will pass over you" (Ex.12:13). God viewed the blood of a substitute lamb and committed Himself to show mercy. This divine prerogative underlies all our considerations of the 'blood of His cross'.

Fortunately, the sight of blood generally indicates injury rather than death. But the word bloodshed implies slaughter. So when Scripture speaks of 'shedding of blood' it always refers to the violent taking of life. That is why, in imposing the death penalty God said, "Whoever sheds man's blood, by man his blood shall be shed" (Gen.9:6). The Hebrew word for shed literally means 'to spill forth'. So bloodshed can obviously cause a person or animal to bleed to death, though it includes violent taking of life generally.

Now as regards the dreadful sufferings of Christ, we know that His back was torn by the cruel lash, His brow was lacerated by the jagged thorns and His hands and feet were pierced by huge nails. From all these wounds His precious blood flowed, as Isaac Watts moving hymn says: *See from His head, His hands, His feet, Sorrow and love flow mingled down.* But 'the blood of His cross' means much more, it is His blood *shed.* So, as we've seen, it is His very life gone forth from Him through violent means. Not taken, however, as men intended, but wondrously given in amazing love. This equating of the Lord's shed blood with His life follows the principle God gave to Noah: "You shall not eat flesh with its life, that is, its blood" (Genesis 9:4).

So the ban on taking human life was accompanied by a ban on the consumption of blood. To understand the reason for this we must first go back to Cain and Abel when God demonstrated that He can only accept sinful man on the basis of a sacrifice involving bloodshed. This principle was more fully expressed in the wide range of sacrifices ordained by Mosaic Law. Leviticus 5:11-13 provided the concession that a very poor person might bring the tenth part of an ephah of fine flour as a sin offering, which explains the precisely accurate statement in Hebrews 9:22

in the Revised Version: "And according to the law, I may almost say, all things are cleansed with blood". However, that merciful provision by no means altered the general principle that "apart from shedding of blood there is no remission."

Upon this principle God opened the way for individuals, and ultimately His people, to enjoy His favour and serve Him acceptably. This involved a system of sacrifices and offerings to which a previous contributor has helpfully drawn our attention. Now the differing requirements regarding the blood of those sacrifices vividly illustrate - albeit inadequately – the precious aspects of 'the blood of His cross' as we shall see. Meanwhile, we draw attention to the fundamental statement God made when instituting the sacrifices referred to. He said, "the life of the flesh is in the blood, and I have given it to you upon the altar ..., for it is the blood that makes atonement for the soul. Therefore I said ... 'No one among you shall eat blood'" (Lev.17:11,12).

Yes, blood was sacred because it represented the cost God demanded to satisfy His judgement against sin, and it anticipated His spotless Son paying the full price. This anticipation was vital for it was "not possible that the blood of bulls and goats could take away sins" (Heb.10:4). Atonement in any age would ultimately depend on Christ's "one sacrifice for sins forever" (Heb.10:12). Then indeed, 'all the accumulated sins of the centuries under the old covenant, which had only been covered by animal sacrifices in anticipation of Calvary, were ... dealt with in full and final settlement' (1). As a result, in contrast to the temporary protection for those who sinned, and the rituals of bodily cleansing, Christ's blood has truly achieved 'much more' for us (Heb.9:14) - nothing less, in fact, than "every possible spiritual benefit" (Eph.1:3 J.B. Phillips). No wonder blood is sacred to God!

Before looking briefly at some of these benefits let us reflect on some illustrations of the effectiveness of Christ's shed blood from Old Testament typology. Firstly, an important distinction. The Israelites were redeemed from Egypt by the blood of the Passover lamb. Later, after pledging obedience, they were sprinkled 'with the blood of the covenant' and became God's people (Ex.19:4-8; Ex.24:3-8). 'The blood of sprinkling' was vital to their subsequent service for God. Similarly, in regard to the blood of Christ, the believer is first personally redeemed by His blood on trusting Him as Saviour (Eph.1:7; 1 Pet.1:18,19); but Scripture also speaks of believers knowing the sanctification of the Spirit "unto obedience and sprinkling of the blood of Jesus Christ" (1 Pet.1:2 RV). This answers to the pledged obedience of Israel at Sinai and sprinkling of the blood on the book itself and on all the people (Ex.24:73; Heb.9:18-20). As with Israel under the Old Covenant, when we pledge our faithfulness to the will of God in service together as His people, we are viewed by Him as having been sprinkled with the blood of Christ to sanctify us for spiritual service - 'the blood of the covenant' wherewith we have been sanctified (Heb.10:29). These different aspects of the application of the blood must be distinguished to avoid serious misunderstanding of Biblical teaching, concerning respectively our personal security and collective responsibility.

Let's now consider the daily burnt offerings - wholly for God, yet paramount for the people. The victim's blood was sprinkled on the altar on all sides four square - all for God from all directions. A vivid illustration of the perfect human life of the Infinite Son completely yielded up in sacrifice to His Father; and totally sufficient to become both the means and the theme of true worship, even from those in 'the four corners of the earth'. Now to some instances from the sin offering. If the priest, or the whole congregation sinned, sacrificial blood was sprinkled seven times before the veil, illustrating that Christ's blood effects complete cleansing for those serving God in His house. Blood was also applied to the horns of the beautiful golden altar of incense, which symbolizes the glory and fragrance of Christ in constant communion with His Father, presenting His people's prayers and praises.

These are acceptable to God who looks on His Son and always has before Him His sin-cleansing blood - not our sin! The remaining blood was poured out on the ground at the copper altar, the place of sacrifice. Yes, Christ's precious blood was freely poured out, as it were, to meet the needs of sinners of earth, as well as saints in the Sanctuary! Now there are at least ten different New Testament terms for Christ's blood (e.g. 'The blood of the Lamb') and as we know every word of Scripture is divinely chosen. We therefore believe that each difference has significance though we may not yet appreciate its precise nature in every case. It has, for example, been suggested that some of the terms indicate different aspects of Christ's death answering to the Levitical offerings. Space does not permit an exploration of this idea which you may find helpful to pursue at your leisure.

Finally, we list some of the treasured blessings attributed by scripture to the blood of Christ:

1. Eternal life: "Whoever ... drinks My blood has eternal life" (Jn.6:54). What a gift. What a cost!

2. Redemption: "redeemed ... with the precious blood of Christ" (1 Pet.1:18,19). Set free - yet bought!

3. Justification: "justified by His blood" (Rom.5:9). Counted righteous in God's sight!

4. Forgiveness and Cleansing: "My blood ... poured out for many for the forgiveness of sins" (Matt.26:28

NIV), "the blood of Jesus ... cleanses us from all sin" (1 Jn.1:7). Sins paid for and continued fellowship provided for!

5. Reconciliation: "to reconcile all things to Himself ... having made peace through the blood of His cross" (Col.1:20). Once enemies, we are now God's friends!

6. Nearness: "once ... far off ... made near by the blood of Christ" (Eph.2:13). As hymnwriter C. Paget puts it:

"So nigh, so very nigh to God,

I cannot nearer be:

For in the person of His Son

I am as near as He."

7. Sanctification: "Jesus ... that He might sanctify the people with His own blood suffered outside the gate" (Heb.13:12).

8. Access: "having boldness to enter the Holiest by the blood of Jesus ... let us draw near" (Heb.10:19-22).

This, our crucial last theme, will be developed in a later chapter. We would just say that the contrast could not be greater between the old once in the year access for a solitary man carrying the blood of a bull and goat into an earthly sanctuary, and the frequent access of a people following the Man who "through His own blood" (Heb.9:12 RV) abides continually in the heavenly sanctuary! In concluding then, may we not only rejoice that our sins are all forgiven, but with God's people; may we ever enjoy our access to the Most Holy Place above. Both these blessings, and many more were brought at infinite cost - 'the blood of His cross'.

> "No longer far from Him, but now
>
> By precious blood made nigh.
>
> Accepted in the Well-beloved,
>
> Near to God's heart we lie."

(1) Terrell, J. D. Needed Truth 1997, p.159.

(Biblical quotations from the NKJV except where otherwise indicated)

CHAPTER FOUR: THE WORD OF THE CROSS (GREG NEELY)

Is it foolishness, or the power of God? It depends on your acceptance of it. "For the word of the cross is to those who are perishing foolishness, but to us who are being saved it is the power of God ... we preach Christ crucified ... Christ the power of God and the wisdom of God" (1 Cor.1:18,23,24).

Paul was set apart for the gospel of God (Rom.1:1). His message was not simply that men should be saved to serve God with individual initiative, but to embrace the whole purpose of God in service in the house of God by a people gathered to the Lord and by the Lord (Acts 20:25,27). Uniquely set apart on the Damascus road for service (though from God's perspective, 'from my mother's womb', according to Galatians 1:15), this apostle did not want people to follow him, but to follow Christ. He baptized few so that none should say he was baptized in Paul's name. But he preached Christ crucified. He taught the doctrine of the Lord, subsequently known as the apostles' teaching and the truth, and declared to Timothy that it is "... God our Saviour, who desires all men to be saved and come to the knowledge of the truth" (1 Tim.2:3,4).

He told Titus about "... our great God and Saviour, Christ Jesus; who gave Himself for us, that He might redeem us from every lawless deed and purify for Himself a people for His own possession, zealous for good deeds. These things speak and exhort and reprove with all authority. Let no one disregard you" (Titus 2:13-15). The word of the Cross is Christ crucified so that He might redeem and purify a people for His own possession as a present experience on earth, and then subsequently throughout eternity. Such a word has authority and must not be disregarded by those who hear.

Cleverness of speech will not bring men to acknowledgement of their sin and their need for the Saviour. 'Your faith should not rest on the wisdom of men, but on the power of God' (1 Cor.2:5). It is pointing to the Person of Christ, hanging on a Cross, who "... Himself bore our sins in His body on the cross, that we might die to sin and live to righteousness; for by His wounds you were healed" (1 Pet.2:24). It is in preaching the gospel "that the cross of Christ should not be made void" (1 Cor.1:17). So Paul writes to the Church of God at Rome and asks: "And how shall they believe in Him whom they have not heard? And how shall they hear without a preacher? And how shall they preach unless they are sent? ... So faith comes from hearing, and hearing by the word (Greek: 'rhema' - spoken word) of Christ" (Rom.10:14,15,17).

Paul's epistle to the Church of God in Rome takes up this grand theme of the Cross of the Lord Jesus and explains in chapter 3 that the righteousness of God has been manifested apart from the Law, the righteousness of God through faith in Jesus Christ for all those who believe. All have sinned; there are no exceptions! All have fallen short of the glory of God; there are no exceptions! Justification (being made righteous) comes not from the Law, but as a gift "... by His grace through the redemption which is in Christ Jesus; whom God displayed publicly as a propitiation in His blood through faith" (vv.24,25).

Our justification before God is secured, not because of what we do, but rather in spite of it by the redemption which is in Christ Jesus. He has been publicly displayed by God as the way in which He can show the sinner mercy. because His justice has been satisfied in Christ's blood shed at Calvary. So He remains just, not accepting sin, nor making any room for it in those He loves, and also the justifier of those who have faith in (or, more likely 'of') Jesus. "In Him we have redemption through His blood, the forgiveness of our trespasses, according to the riches of His grace, which He lavished upon us ..." (Eph.1:7).

So, Paul goes on to tell the Corinthians, "If any man is in Christ, he is a new creature ... Now all these things are from God, who reconciled us to Himself through Christ, and gave us the ministry of reconciliation, namely, that God was in Christ reconciling the world to Himself, not counting their trespasses against them ..." (2 Cor.5:17-19). The ministry which has been given to disciples of the Lord Jesus is that reconciliation, that is, preaching the word of the Cross. That is what brings a person to God. God is never spoken of as being reconciled to man. That is not necessary. But man is reconciled to God for it is God whose standard has been broken and of whose glory we have fallen short.

Reconciliation involves a change in relationships with God, because our trespasses are no longer counted against us. Had there been no Saviour on the Cross, they would have been. But they all have been forgiven and the certificate of debt consisting of decrees against us and which was hostile to us has been cancelled: "He has taken it out of the way, having nailed it to the cross" (Col.2:14). No wonder Paul can say, "I am not ashamed of the gospel, for it is the power of God for salvation to everyone who believes, to the Jew first and also to the Greek. For in it the righteousness of God is revealed from faith to faith ..." (Rom.1:16,17).

Faith is the means by which this word of the Cross is received by the sinner who is deserving of the wrath of God, and on whom the wrath of God abides (Jn.3:36). But upon his acceptance of it by faith, "There is therefore now no condemnation for those who are in Christ Jesus ... for what the Law could not do, weak as it was through the flesh, God did: sending His own Son in the likeness of sinful flesh and as an offering for sin, He condemned sin in the flesh" (Rom.8:1,3). From sinner under wrath, bound by a certificate of debt and under condemnation, to saint set free and set apart for holy living, such is the power of God through the gospel to everyone who believes.

The word of the Cross depends upon the blood of the Cross from the Man of the Cross. If Jesus were just a man, then indeed the word of the Cross would be foolishness, for the blood of the Cross would be sinful blood, and there could be no salvation in it. If he were just a dead human, "then our preaching is vain, your faith also is vain ... your faith is worthless; you are still in your sins" (1 Cor.15:14,17). But He is God the Son, manifest in the flesh, the One in whom dwells all the fulness of the Godhead in bodily form. The Man of the Cross is the Man whom "God raised ... up again, putting an end to the agony of death, since it was impossible for Him to be held in its power" (Acts 2:24); the blood of the Cross is "precious blood, as of a lamb unblemished and spotless, the blood of Christ" (1 Pet.1:19); and the word of the Cross is the power of God.

Some reject the word; some accept it. "But thanks be to God, who always leads us in His triumph in Christ, and manifests through us the sweet aroma of the knowledge of Him in every place. For we are a fragrance of Christ to God among those who are being saved and among those who are perishing; to the one an aroma from death to death, to the other an aroma from life to life" (2 Cor.2:14-16). Is it not a delightful privilege to be a fragrance of Christ to God? It is encouraging for the faithful saint who speaks the word of the Cross with little evidence of fruit, that no matter what the result (which is in God's hands in any case) there is a sweet fragrance of Christ to God.

To the one who rejects Christ the aroma is to death. To the one who accepts Him, the aroma is to life. No wonder Paul told Timothy: "Preach the word; be ready in season and out of season; reprove, rebuke, exhort, with great patience and instruction" (2 Tim.4:2). We'd all love to have results such as Peter had on the day of Pentecost when 3,000 responded to the word of the Cross and the Church of God in Jerusalem exploded in size and power. But if that is not our experience, we still preach with great patience and instruction. For in it is the power of God!

Teachers with wrong doctrine and little appreciation of Christ's finished work at Calvary were leading the Galatians astray, advising them to obey aspects of the Law rather than relying solely on God's grace. They wanted to avoid persecution which accompanied the word of the Cross of Christ. As a result, they wanted to boast to the Jewish leaders about the circumcision of men in the churches of Galatia, according to the Law. "But may it never be that I should boast, except in the cross of our Lord Jesus Christ, through which the world has been crucified to me and I to the world" (Gal.6:14).

The word of the Cross is neither dependent on our adherence to the Law, nor circumcision of flesh. It is Christ and Him crucified. It is the means by which the world is crucified to the believer and the believer to the world. There is nothing else which can make such a dramatic transformation in a person's life and character. "He died for all, that they who live should no longer live for themselves, but for Him who died and rose again on their behalf" (2 Cor.5:15).

For whom are you living, who have heard the word of the Cross and accepted the One of whom is speaks? "For many walk ... enemies of the cross of Christ ... who set their minds on earthly things" (Phil.3:18,19). Conversely, the word of the Cross in the Spirit-led believer brings him to say with Paul: "I have been crucified with Christ; and it is no longer I who live, but Christ lives in me; and the life which I now live in the flesh I live by faith in the Son of God, who loved me, and delivered Himself up for me" (Gal.2:20). What is your response to the word of the Cross?

CHAPTER FIVE: LET HIM DENY HIMSELF (PHIL CAPEWELL)

'Taking up his cross'

"Then Jesus said to His disciples, 'If anyone desires to come after Me, let him deny himself, and take up his cross, and follow Me'" (Matt.16:24). In every reference to this statement of the Lord, Matthew 16:24, Mark 8:34, and Luke 9:23, the setting is the same; it is set against the background of the Lord's declaration of His own death. Like all good leaders, yet outstanding above them all, He would not call on His followers to do anything which he was not prepared to do Himself. During one of history's great marches, Alexander the Great and his troops were desperate for water. Some Macedonians, having fetched water from a river, came across the leader choking with thirst under the midday sun. They poured water into a helmet and offered it to him, but seeing his men equally desperate for a drink, he handed it back without tasting a drop. 'For,' he explained, 'if I alone should drink, the rest would lose heart'. His soldiers, inspired by the self-sacrifice of their leader, were immediately galvanized into action to continue the pursuit of the enemy.

In life's onward march, surely we need to look no further than our matchless Leader, "For even Christ did not please Himself" (Rom.15:3). In our willing pursuit of the path of self-denial, we follow the Man who one day offered His scourged shoulders and back to the weight of the Cross. It was this exemplary self-denial that inspired Jim Elliot's short life: 'Father, let me be weak that I might loose my clutch on everything temporal. My life, my reputation, my possessions, Lord, let me lose the tensions of the grasping hand. Even, Father, would I lose the love of *fondling*. How often have I released a grasp only to retain what I prized by "harmless" longing, the fondling touch. Rather, open my Hand ... as Christ's hand was opened – that I, releasing all, might be released, unleashed from all that binds me now. He thought Heaven, yea equality with God, not a thing to be clutched at. So let me release my grasp" (1).

Glorying in the Cross

"But far be it from me to glory, save in the cross of our Lord Jesus Christ, through whom the world hath been crucified unto me, and I unto the world" (Gal.6:14 RV margin). In Paul's sight, the Cross marked the end of his association with the world. He turned away from it with distaste, as from a crucified malefactor. The world was crucified to him; he disdained its attractions, systems, friendships and religions. Equally, he was dead to the world. There could be no compromise in his life that would allow him to enter the evil world which had rejected Christ and crucified Him. As it had no place for his Lord, it had no place for him. Paul's rule of life should be ours too.

"Nay, world! I turn away,

Though thou seem fair and good;

That friendly outstretched hand of thine

Is stained with Jesus' blood.

If in thy least device

I stoop to take a part,

All unaware, thine influence steals

Gods presence from my heart."

(Margaret Mauro)

Apparently, there were some in the churches in Galatia who urged the Christians to be circumcised in order that they themselves might escape the persecution which was associated with the Cross of Christ and that they might boast about the Christians acceding to their request. But, to Paul, there was no glory in such pointless conformity. There was only one thing in which he would glory - the Cross of Christ. Its recurrent theme in his epistle to the Galatians shows its importance to this scarred warrior. In Galatian 2:20, he had written, "I have been crucified with Christ; it is no longer I who live, but Christ lives in me; and the life which I now live in the flesh I live by faith in the Son of God, who loved me and gave Himself for me".

Saul of Tarsus was dead, Paul the apostle was alive. As a sinner, he had been under the death penalty, but the Son of God gave Himself up for him. In the crucifixion of Christ, Saul saw an end to his old sinful self, but in the resurrection of Christ he saw himself quickened by a new life. Christ was in him, living His life over again in His persecuted servant. He urged the Corinthians to the same necessary sequence of death and life "... always carrying about in the body the dying of ... Jesus, that the life of Jesus also may be manifested in our body" (2 Cor.4:10). Surely this finest of all possibilities challenges us too, the potential for the life of Jesus to be manifested in our mortal flesh (v.11).

They ... have crucified the flesh

Then, in Galatians 5:24, he said, "And they that are of Christ Jesus have crucified the flesh with the passions and lusts thereof" (RV). Noting carefully Paul's use here of the term 'of Christ Jesus', we recognize the sad possibility of believers *in* Christ Jesus falling prey to the ever-present evil of the flesh. But those who are 'of Christ Jesus' have themselves crucified the flesh with its passions and desires, an action which is a necessary addendum to walking by the Spirit. This is a two-sided approach, we must crucify the flesh, repudiating what we know is wrong, but we must also "walk by the Spirit", deliberately setting ourselves to follow His initiative. We are not to show any pity to the flesh. Crucifixion was a shameful, pitiless death reserved for the worst criminals, and, because it is so thoroughly evil, we are to crucify the flesh.

Though crucifixion was slow and lingering, it was decisive. Criminals who were nailed to a cross were left there to die. Soldiers were even stationed at the scene to ensure that there was no escape of any kind. The appeal of the flesh may take different forms today from what it did in the apostle's day, but it is to be dealt with just as ruthlessly and decisively. Crucifixion is final. There must be no tampering with the flesh, no wistful longing for its release. In the Lord's words, we must take up the cross daily, not just walking with it, but carrying it to the place of execution. We must take the wilful, sinful flesh and nail it to the cross, repudiating it utterly each day.

Enemies of the Cross of Christ

"For many walk, of whom I have told you often, and now tell you even weeping, that they are enemies of the cross of Christ" (Phil.3:18). In every age there are good examples and bad. Here, Paul asks the church to mark those who are imitators of him and make them their goal for, he says, there are others who make gluttony their lifestyle. Such people are "enemies of the cross of Christ" in the sense that they are setting aside the truth of Paul's words in Galatians 2:20, "I have been crucified with Christ; it is no longer I who live, but Christ lives in me". Here is true Christian living! It is the living expression of the fact that Christ not only died *for us,* but that we died *with Him.* To Paul, all the old fleshly appetites were dead and so he calls on the Philippians to follow his example, as opposed to these misguided persons who overindulged themselves to such an extent that their god was their belly.

The Offence of the Cross

Paul preached Christ crucified (1 Cor.1:23), though it cost him severe persecution. It seems from Galatians 5:11, that those who taught a return to the rites of the Law had actually dared to claim Paul as championing their opinions. They were reporting him as being an advocate of circumcision. Paul denies the claim, reasoning that if he preached circumcision he would not be enduring persecution. Circumcision itself may not be the issue today, but that of which it speaks, a reliance on human achievement, is by many much preferred to the message of the Cross. The true message of the Cross completely rules out any supposed spiritual blessing through the works of the flesh (Rom.3:20).

The preaching of 'circumcision', human achievement, is a much more comfortable message. It is inoffensive. Save yourselves by your own good deeds. To preach Christ crucified is to state clearly to people that they are sinners under God's condemnation, that they cannot do anything to save themselves and that only through Christ crucified can they be saved. That gospel is offensive to people's pride. Today's tolerant society would prefer us to tone down the message of the Cross, telling us that it doesn't matter what people believe as long as they're sincere. The Christian message differs vastly from that and, like Paul, we must not shrink from it, though it is unpopular. A 'gospel' of human achievement would find much more general acceptance than the Cross of Christ. Though it cause offence and invite persecution, we must determine to 'preach ... the Cross'.

"The cross of Christ is all my boast,

His blood my only plea;

My password to the realms of bliss,

Is, Jesus died for me."

(Author unknown)

(1) Elliot, E. 1958 *Shadow of the Almighty* p.59 Hodder and Stoughton.

(Biblical quotations from the NKJV except where otherwise stated)

CHAPTER SIX: REDEEMED AT THE CROSS (JOHN KERR)

Israel's Expectations

We begin by asking ourselves what were the expectations of those, who along with Anna, were described by Luke as looking for the redemption of Jerusalem'? (Lk.2:36-38). These people clearly looked for Israel's promised Messiah; hoping that one day soon He would deliver their nation from Roman bondage. It is very doubtful whether they would understand that the redemption they looked forward to would include the death of their Messiah on a Roman cross. As history unfolded, those who outlived the death and resurrection of Jesus, would have the opportunity to experience the benefits of a much greater plan of redemption than they could ever have anticipated.

The Believer's Redemption

Not many years later, another group of people were able to look back and say with Paul about Christ, "In whom we have our redemption through his blood" (Eph.1:7). They had come to appreciate the spiritual redemption that was bought for them at infinite cost. They perceived, as we do also, that the main reason for this same Messiah coming was that He might die on a Roman cross for the purpose of providing this redemption. Compared to Old Testament saints therefore, we have a richer and fuller understanding of this great truth.

Our Redeemer

What exactly is redemption? Putting it another way, what constitutes a redeemer? In its simplest form the dictionary meaning is one who buys back. It appears that from earliest times it was common knowledge that it involved deliverance from some sort of bondage on payment of a price. God's servant Job said, "I know that my redeemer liveth" (Job 19:25) and from this we learn that Job's resurrection hopes were centred in God, who he knew in some way would save him from the eternal penalty of his sins and bring him back to Himself. In the New Testament many scriptures focus on Christ as our redeemer, emphasizing the price of our redemption and explaining the crucial part that His death on the Cross had to play in it.

This is clearly taught by Peter who states in his first epistle that we are "redeemed, not with corruptible things, with silver or gold ... but with precious blood, as of a lamb without blemish and without spot, even the blood of Christ" (1 Pet.1:18,19). So Christ achieved our redemption, having delivered us from divine judgement by paying the price God demanded, the shedding of His blood on the Cross. However, through the shed blood of our Saviour much more has been assured to us; the blessings of the New Covenant, for example, and many other assured truths revealed in the New Testament. To some of these we now turn our attention and notice how they affect the people of God collectively rather than ourselves individually.

The Blood of the Covenant

Come with me now to the Upper Room scene where our Lord gathered with His disciples for the last time before He suffered. In retrospect we can readily appreciate why the outpouring of the cup of wine at the Lord's supper is so important as a symbol of the shedding of His blood at Calvary. When He said, "This cup is the new covenant in my blood" (Lk.22:20). He was in a few words reminding us of the many blessings of the New Covenant, and at the same time highlighting the cost to Himself of making these benefits available.

When Israel entered into covenant relationship with God as His people, Moses took the blood of calves and goats and sprinkled it upon the book of the Law and the people, and also upon the Tabernacle and its vessels (Heb.9:18-21). They became the people of the book, pledged to obey its laws, and their service to God was centred in the Tabernacle, His dwelling place on earth. Under the terms of the new covenant our sins are permanently forgiven as far as eternal judgement is concerned, and God's people are invited to enter into the heavenly sanctuary, the holy place above, by "obedience and sprinkling of the blood of Jesus Christ" as Peter expresses it in his first epistle (1 Pet.1:2). Thus cleansed and in tune with God, His laws written on our hearts and minds, we "draw near with a true heart in fulness of faith" (Heb.10:14-23). This is one of the great privileges assured to us on account of His shed blood.

A Peculiar People

To this aspect of redemption, the redemption of a people for God, Paul refers in Titus 2:13,14 to "... our great God and Saviour Jesus Christ; who gave himself for us, that he might redeem us from all iniquity, and purify unto himself a people for his own possession, zealous of good works". We can see it affects our present daily living. Commenting on this verse Bible expositor John Miller helpfully states:

'Jehovah in a past dispensation redeemed Israel, so that they should be to Him a peculiar treasure. He said, "If ye will obey my voice indeed, and keep my covenant, then ... ye shall be unto me a kingdom of priests, and an holy nation" (Ex.19:5,6). Similarly

today, but on a higher plane, the Lord gave Himself
for us, not merely to redeem us from past sin', but
from present lawlessness, that is, from doing our own
will and being a law unto ourselves, and to purify unto
Himself a peculiar (that is, excellent) people. The
character and conduct of this people is to be "zealous
of good works". To many saved folk the thought of
God having a people is not in their thoughts. To
many, evangelism fills entirely their thoughts and
time, but God's will is that He should have a peculiar
people, a subject people under the authority of the
Lord, who is our great God and Saviour Jesus Christ'
(1).

A Praising People

God's plan of redemption takes care of all our spiritual needs.
The ransom price has been completely paid on our behalf. God
has accepted Christ's sacrifice as payment in full. Everything
about it therefore is to His glory. "Through him then let us offer
up a sacrifice of praise to God continually, that is, the fruit of lips
which make confession to his name" (Heb.13:15). Those who
take their place among the people of God by acknowledging
Christ as Lord and obeying His word, He has made "a kingdom,
priests unto his God and Father" (Rev.1:6) and the service of a
holy priesthood is "to offer up spiritual sacrifices, acceptable to
God through Jesus Christ" (1 Pet.2:5). Should this not occupy
much more of our thought and attention? Should there not pour
out from our redeemed hearts continual praise in appreciation of
what the Lord Jesus has accomplished through the shedding of
His blood?

The Song of the Redeemed

We cannot bring this chapter to a close without a reminder about the future glories of Christ, presented in the Revelation as the exalted Lamb of God. Redemption by His blood will obviously be the theme of heaven's praise throughout eternal ages. The redeemed of every nation will join with heavenly beings in swelling the praise of Him who once was slain upon the tree. "And they sing a new song, saying, Worthy art thou ... for thou wast slain, and didst purchase unto God with thy blood men of every tribe, and tongue, and people, and nation, and madest them to be unto our God a kingdom and priests ... Worthy is the Lamb that hath been slain to receive the power, and riches, and wisdom, and might, and honour, and glory, and blessing" (Rev.5:9-12).

(1) Miller, J. Notes on the Epistles, p.434, Hayes Press

CHAPTER SEVEN: THE WAY OF THE CROSS (ALAN TOMS)

"If any man would come after Me, let him deny himself, and take up his cross daily, and follow Me" (Lk.9:23). The context in which these words are set is most significant. The great declaration of Caesarea Philippi had just been made. The mystery which had been hid from all ages and generations was now revealed, that Christ was to build His Church, against which the gates of Hades would never prevail. And the scripture says "from that time began Jesus to shew unto His disciples, how that He must go unto Jerusalem, and suffer many things of the elders and chief priests and scribes, and be killed! and the third day be raised up".

This Church was to be born out of suffering. The fact that their Master must suffer was completely new to the disciples, and they found it hard to receive. Their cherished hope was that He would restore the kingdom to Israel. They expected to see Him on a throne, not upon a cross. They had yet to learn that the way to the throne was via the cross. It was a hard lesson to learn in regard to their Master, and there was another, equally hard, which concerned themselves, for the Lord Jesus went on to speak the weighty words which we are considering together.

The Lord Jesus must suffer. There was no other way for Him. And if any man would come after Him, there is no other way for that man. "Let him deny himself". The strong "I" which so constantly asserts itself, and which loves its own way, must be denied. And let him "take up his cross daily". A cross is for dying on. It has no other purpose. The Master clearly taught that every one who would come after Him must be prepared to die to self each day, and so to follow Him. These are stern words which touch us deeply if we love the Lord Jesus and desire above all else to follow Him. We may well ask ourselves what exactly is involved. Help may be gleaned from references to the cross in the writings of the apostles and we refer to three of them.

Weakness

In Second Corinthians the cross is associated with weakness. "He was crucified through weakness, yet He liveth through the power of God" (2 Corinthians 13:4). If the Lord Jesus was weary when He sat by Sychar's well, how much more weary must He have been when early in the morning of that Passover day they laid a heavy cross upon His back and led Him to Calvary. The help which Simon of Cyrene was compelled to give was doubtless necessitated by His extreme bodily weakness. Yet the "weakness" of the incarnate Christ included much more than physical weariness. But out of that weakness came power, for "He liveth through the power of God".

Power is made perfect in weakness; not an easy lesson to learn, as Paul found in his experience. Three times he besought the Lord concerning his thorn in the flesh, and the answer he received was different from that for which he had hoped, but in accepting it he found it was for his highest good. Indeed, not only did he accept his weakness but he learned to glory in it. "Wherefore I take pleasure in weaknesses ... for Christ's sake" he wrote, "for when I am weak, then am I strong". The power of Christ spread a tabernacle over human weakness.

Weakness (Greek: asthenes) is a relative word. We might be weak and have a little strength, but this is a word which means totally without strength. "While we were yet weak, in due season Christ died for the ungodly" (Rom.5:6). We know that the sinner is entirely without strength to save himself. And the servant of Christ has to learn that of himself he is entirely without strength to serve the Lord. "Apart from Me ye can do nothing" He said. Paul learned it, and we must learn it, too. This is the way of the cross. "Pressed ... perplexed ... pursued ... smitten down ... always bearing about in the body the dying of Jesus, that the life also of Jesus may be manifested in our body".

Suffering

Peter in his first epistle refers to the cross of the Lord Jesus in connection with His suffering for well-doing. "Christ also suffered for you, leaving you an example, that ye should follow His steps: who did no sin, neither was guile found in His mouth" (1 Pet.2:21,22). Many of the household servants to whom he wrote were suffering for well-doing, suffering simply because they were Christians, and not ashamed to acknowledge the fact. The inference is that some of them were buffeted for Christ's sake. "Buffeted" is a strong word, meaning to strike with the fist. They did it to the Master. "Then did they spit in His face and buffet Him" (Matt.26:67). They clenched their fists and struck Him until "His visage was so marred more than any man". And when Peter wrote his epistle many were called to be partakers of Christ's sufferings. Not His vicarious sufferings - these could never be shared but His suffering in association with the cross, "as it is written, the reproaches of, them that reproached Thee fell upon Me". There is a reproach associated with the cross which the disciple must not expect to escape. "Yea, and all that would live godly in Christ Jesus shall suffer persecution".

Death

Each epistle presents a different aspect of the cross of Christ, and in Galatians crucifixion and death are emphasized to us. Whether it is the world which presents its claims, or the flesh with its strong appeal, the cross is the only answer. Men would make a fair show in the flesh, but God says it is corrupt and the only place for it is death upon the cross. That was the secret of Paul's life, and his memorable words stand on record for the help of disciples through all time.

"I have been crucified with Christ; yet I live; and yet no longer I, but Christ liveth in me: and that life which I now live in the flesh I live in faith, the faith which is in the Son of God, who loved me, and gave Himself up for me" (Gal.2:20). "Christ liveth in me". How our hearts respond to the possibility. The life of Jesus manifested in our mortal bodies. How is it possible? Romans 6:11 supplies the answer. "Reckon ye also yourselves to be dead unto sin, but alive unto God in Christ Jesus". It is to be a daily reckoning. "I die daily" cried the apostle. "Take up his cross daily" taught the Master. And if we do so Christ will live His resurrection life in us, as surely as the new life of Spring bursts out of the death of winter.

"Reckon, reckon, reckon,

Reckon rather than feel:

Let us be true to the reckoning,

And God will make it real".

Weakness, suffering, death! This is a stern word indeed. By nature we shrink from such things. And the great adversary whispers; "be it far from Thee ... this shall never be unto Thee". But the Master calls us to follow where He has led. And we know that He never calls but for our highest good. It is earthly loss set against heavenly gain, and each disciple must count the cost for himself. In our accounting let us remember that there is only one possible answer to the timeless question, which was addressed originally to disciples, and not to the unsaved, "what shall a man be profited, if he shall gain the whole world, and forfeit his life?" Our crucified and exalted Master still calls the way of the cross.

CHAPTER EIGHT: JESUS' WORDS FROM THE CROSS (REG DARKE)

"Father, forgive them" (Lk.23:34)

Death by crucifixion was first conceived by the Phoenicians, and copied by Rome. Stoning was Israel's punishment; yet the piercing of the hands and feet of the Lord was a fulfilment of prophecy (Ps.22:16; Jn.19:37). The wooden cross, or stake, was laid on the ground, and the soldiers wrestled the victim into a prostrate position on it. His hands and feet were held forcibly in place as the spikes were ruthlessly driven into the flesh, binding the victim to the wood.

> "Hark, I hear the dull blow
>
> Of the hammer swung blow,
>
> They are nailing my Lord to the tree."

"And it was the third hour and they crucified Him" (Mk.15:25). How amazed the soldiers must have been by the gentle, willing, and completely unresisting attitude of the Lord Jesus! No reviling, only a heart-rending, prayerful cry, "Father, forgive them; for they know not what they do". What a marked contrast He is to all others! How He stands out so nobly, so majestically! And His cry was of forgiveness! Was it for His executioners? Or was the plea to heaven's Throne for His own people? Or was it a universal prayer of forgiveness? The Lord predicted that the Jews would deliver Him to the Gentiles for crucifixion (Matt.20:19); and the early disciples distinguished between "Herod and Pontius Pilate, with the Gentiles and peoples of Israel", being gathered together against the Lord Jesus. It was all part of the prophetic fulfilment in its embracing of the Gentiles and the kings of the earth (Acts 4:25-28). None then, need be exempt from the Saviour's plea for forgiveness. The living words contain the divine power for saving any man's soul.

"Today shalt thou be with Me in Paradise" (Lk.23:43)

Callous indifference; cruel mocking; scoffing and taunting, all contributed to the tense atmosphere which built up around the Cross whilst, untouched by the excruciating pain endured by the crucified, the Jewish rulers vented their spleen on the Lord Jesus. "He saved others: let Him save Himself, if this is the Christ of God, His Chosen", they shouted. The soldiers joined them taunting, "If Thou art the King of the Jews, save Thyself" (Lk.23:37). The two robbers added their chorus of reproaches, but the Lord quietly suffered it all (Matt.27:44). Then followed a dialogue between the two thieves which resulted in one condemning and the other defending the Saviour. "This Man", the one exclaimed, "hath done nothing amiss". What an awakening! What a discovery! It led to his salvation. He realized that the Man in the midst was the King. With newly found faith he cried, "Jesus, remember me when Thou comest in Thy kingdom". Instantly came the reply of total forgiveness and eternal hope, "Today shalt thou be with Me in Paradise" (Lk.23:39-43). Only the Eternal One could make such a promise and fulfil it.

"Woman, behold, thy son! ... Behold, thy mother!" (Jn.19:26,27)

A strange assortment of humanity was drawn, as by a magnet, to that "Green hill ... outside the city wall". Those who enjoy the gruesome joined those who scorned; and those who were intrigued by the spectacular end to the gentle Man who performed miracles, and who spoke kindly words, might have stood sympathetically with those who loved the One on the middle cross. The location of Peter is not recorded. There were some disciples who stood afar off. Is it the fear of identification with Him which causes this, or the physical inability to cope with the close-up view of a loved One enduring prolonged grief and pain? Neither deterred the faithful women, who held silent, loving vigil with John, so close to the suffering Saviour. John records: "But there were standing by the Cross of Jesus His mother, and His mother's sister, Mary the wife of Clopas, and Mary Magdalene. When Jesus therefore saw His mother, and the disciple standing by, whom He loved, He saith unto His mother, Woman, behold, thy Son! Then saith He to the disciple, Behold, thy mother! And from that hour the disciple took her unto his own home" (Jn.19:25-27).

Mary had been chosen by God from among all women to give birth to the Christ-child. Her eyes must have filled with tears of joy when she first nestled the Babe in her arms. She had been highly honoured by heaven in the care, the feeding of, and in providing for, the young Child, the Youth and the growing Man. And now in His closing hours she beholds Him hanging on the accursed Cross. No tears of joy in this scene, but many of grief and sorrow. How the deep emotions of a mother's love must have flooded her soul as she looked on His suffering body and pain-wracked yet gracious face. The moment had also now come for her delicate soul to receive the piercing of the sword foretold at His birth, "that thoughts out of many hearts may be revealed" (Lk.2:35). It took the Cross, and words from the Saviour Himself, to reveal to Mary her part in the great divine plan enacted by Him to bring eternal blessing to the human race. He who in early life was sheltered by this dear woman, now makes provision for her before He dies. It was the second of His final bequests. The first was a place in Paradise for the dying thief; and now He committed Mary into the care of John, the beloved, who took her to his home.

"My God, My God, why hast Thou forsaken Me?" (Matt.27:46)

Three hours of excruciating torture have been endured without complaint by God's dear Son. In the light of such intense suffering our redeemed hearts are forced to enquire: "I wonder what He saw in me suffer such deep agony". Mercilessly the sun's rays have beaten down on His defenceless head, intensifying His sufferings; then, mercifully, the sun was obscured and darkness descended upon the whole land.

Can we not see through the eyes of faith that He must know this darkness that we might be saved from the blackness of darkness for ever? He must sink in deep mire, where sin has taken us, that we might know beneath us the strength of the Everlasting Arms. He must know the waves and billows of God's wrath, that we might escape the storm. He must know the fire of God's judgement, that we might be saved from the fires of hell. The blackness, the fury, the fire, were all our due, but He, as our sin-Bearer, endured it all. We deserved to be forsaken by a holy God because of sin, but He willingly took our place.

Mystery of mysteries, that God should forsake His Son! If the burning bush was holy ground for Moses, how much more Calvary to the redeemed heart. Holy ground, burnt ground; for where He was consumed in our place by the fires of God's wrath, we stand protected, knowing that the fire cannot touch that place again.

"'Neath Thy cross I stand and worship,

Suffering Man, yet conquering God!

Resting on Thy death-atonement,

Weary, I lay down my load."

"I thirst" (Jn.19:28)

Out of the prevailing darkness came the Lord's cry, "I thirst". Yet another of the prophetic utterances must be fulfilled. "My strength is dried up like a potsherd; and My tongue cleaveth to My jaws" (Ps.22:15). "I am weary with My crying; My throat is dried" (Ps. 69:3). "And in My thirst they gave Me vinegar to drink" (Ps.69:21). The One who cried to a thirsty nation, "Come unto Me, and drink" (Jn.7:37), Himself knew extreme thirst on the Cross. The One who gave to a needy, sinful woman the water of life, was Himself forced to cry, "I thirst". When He sat at Sychar's well He was weary with His journey and asked the Samaritan woman, "Give Me to drink". "The well is deep" said the Samaritan woman when the Lord spoke of the living water which He would give; but it was not so deep as the well of His suffering on the Cross.

It is about the ninth hour of the crucifixion day when His desperate cry is heard. The end of the battle of all battles is now in sight and the divine Warrior, the Captain of our salvation, longs for a thirst-quenching drink of cool water. The response to His cry, "I thirst" appeared to be immediate; but the callous nature with which man had been imbued by sin, revealed itself in a sponge full of vinegar being pressed to His parched lips. "Marah" might well be written across these closing moments of His sufferings.

"It is finished" (Jn.19:30)

Matthew, Mark and Luke all tell us that the Lord cried out with a loud voice before giving up His spirit. It is John who tells us that He cried, "It is finished". In the Greek it has a ring of triumph about it: Tetelestai! His work of salvation was perfect and complete so that nothing more needs to be done.

In His memorable prayer of review of His earthly labours, the Lord Jesus speaks to His Father as though all things have been accomplished. "I glorified Thee on the earth, having accomplished the work which Thou hast given Me to do" (Jn.17:4). Only a matter of hours awaited the literal fulfilment of His words, when He was to become the great sin-Purger. All the demands of a holy God were met at Calvary. There sin, Satan, and hell were all defeated. Salvation, justification, eternal life are now freely available to every sinful person. One has explained that the Greek sculptor would cry, "Tetelestai!" when his work was finished; no finishing touches necessary; nothing more needing to be done.

"Christ has done the mighty work;

Nothing left for us to do

But to enter on His toil,

Enter on His triumph too."

"Father, into Thy hands I commend My spirit" (Lk.23:46)

Christ's work upon the Cross began and ended with a cry to His Father. The wondrous eternal relationship remained unbroken. The moment has now come when the waiting Father receives the offered spirit of His Son. Heaven must have been hushed when this remarkable happening took place. Men were waiting to put an end to His life; the Father waited for Him to bow His holy head and dismiss His spirit. Voluntarily He laid down His life; voluntarily He gave up the ghost. No man took His life from Him. The soldier pierced His side, and out flowed blood and water. A centurion glorified God saying, "Certainly this was a righteous Man" (Lk.23:47). And the closing scenes reveal multitudes smiting their breasts when they beheld the things which were done.

"The One who suffered grief and shame

Is raised and glorified.

We sing the triumph of His name,

Who groaned and bled and died."

CHAPTER NINE: CALVARY NAILS (BRIAN JOHNSTON)

A little girl was once asked how she would recognize the Lord Jesus if He were to walk into the room. 'He's got big holes in His hands', was her reply. Those 'big holes' were made by Calvary nails, rough things probably each like six-inch iron stakes. The description John gives of the print of those nails (20:25) employs the same word as that for 'form' (pattern) in "you obeyed from the heart that form of doctrine to which you were delivered" (Rom.6:17). The Lord showed the pattern of the nails in His hands to His disciple who doubted. To all genuine doubters since, the Lord shows the pattern of teaching in His Word by which we serve according to the commission of those same nail-scarred hands (Matt.28:18-20).

In 1 Chronicles 22:3 we discover that there had to be nails for there to be a house of God at Jerusalem at the time of the building of Solomon's Temple. These were nails for its doors and gates. There could be no house without nails. The same is true of Calvary nails. Christ's death (with its piercing, Ps.22:16), also at Jerusalem, was essential to the existence of an earthly house for God today giving access to a heavenly sanctuary.

Hebrews chapter 8 verse 2 speaks of the Lord as minister of that sanctuary above in heaven which is further described as being the true tabernacle which the Lord pitched, not man. This is not a reference to the Tabernacle-tent which Moses pitched on the desert floor, but to something definitely not man-made which exists in heaven. The thing that Moses pitched was only a copy of the great Original. When did the Lord pitch the true tabernacle? Perhaps from the foundation of the world it had stood awaiting a high priest who could bring redeemed humanity in there to worship in spirit.

There is an interesting connection with what Peter said in his maiden sermon in Acts 2:23 when he brought the scenes of the Cross before his audience. He told his Jewish hearers that Jesus had been delivered up by the determined purpose and foreknowledge of God, but that they too had played a part, for by the hands of lawless men they had crucified Him and put Him to death. The word 'crucified' there in Peter's address is from the same original word as the word meaning pitched in the above Hebrews' verse.

At some unspecified time the Lord pitched that original tabernacle-tent in heaven. He pegged it out and made it fast. But it awaited the risen Christ as our High Priest. It must wait until after He came to earth and was Himself pitched full-length on the torture stake at Golgotha; there they pegged Him out on the Cross under the morning sun; making Him fast to the scaffold by cruel Calvary nails. This He willingly endured so that the tent in the heavens might be filled with our praise. In order for it to be so He came to fill Calvary's central Cross. He filled the Cross so that we, while still here as a pilgrim people on the earth, might be able to draw near as worshippers into heaven itself. Week by week that sanctuary in heaven, now as the place of our worship, is filled with our praise as we remember Him who bore those awful Calvary nails.

We have already considered how Christ, as "great priest over the house of God" (Heb.10:21 RV) serves in resurrection in the heavenly tabernacle, of which the Scripture says quite explicitly it was "not made with hands". With reference to this true tabernacle (Heb.8:2; 9:11), we read Christ entered into the most holy place itself of which again it is said that it was 'not made with hands'. If He has entered as a forerunner, what can be said of all who follow after Him to draw near as worshippers? They have known Christ's circumcision of the heart, concerning which Colossians 2:11 says that it too is something 'made without hands'. Those who enter are made answerable to a heavenly environment which is not man-made, but is a work all of God. Yet every time we break the bread we remember that in the will of God all this entailed something that was man-made: the wounds inflicted by cruel Calvary nails.

CHAPTER TEN: THE CROSS FORETOLD – 'THE LAMB SLAIN FROM THE FOUNDATION OF THE WORLD' (BRIAN FULLARTON)

Spontaneously the believer's heart warms to the matchless theme of the Cross of our Lord Jesus Christ! For in the suffering Lamb of Calvary all our spiritual hope is centred. This book is designed to enrich our scriptural appreciation of the mighty work accomplished by our Saviour through His death on the Cross. This chapter explores the astonishing truth that the Cross work was **forethought, foreplanned** and **foredated** in eternal counsels (Acts 2:23).

The Lamb Foreknown

How revealing was the witness of John the Baptist: "He that cometh after me is become before me (in front of, first in place): for he was before me" (first in time) (Jn.1:15). The Lord Jesus Himself declared to disbelieving Jews, "Verily, verily, I say unto you, Before Abraham was, I am" (Jn.8:58). In His prayer recorded in John 17 the Lord also confirmed that He had shared the Father's love before the foundation of the world (verse 24). Even more wonderfully it is revealed in 1 Peter 1:19,20 that before the foundation of the world He was foreknown as the Lamb without a blemish and without spot.

We ponder the deep mystery that in those dateless ages, 'before times eternal', impenetrable divine counsels anticipated the dilemma of a fallen race, and decreed that restoration to God would be made possible by the precious blood of the Lamb. With infinite, supreme wisdom, Deity devised this plan of salvation which involved the crucifixion of the Lord of glory (1 Cor.2:7,8). How could a felon's death be part of the strategy of divine wisdom? Yet this was the means devised to bring many to eternal glory. "Before the foundation of the world' the God and Father of our Lord Jesus Christ chose us in Him" (Eph.1:3,4). His own purpose and grace anticipated the giving of eternal life to all who would be redeemed through His death on the Cross; "given us in Christ Jesus before times eternal" (2 Tim.1:9; Tit.1:2; Rom.16:25).

We may only surmise what deep and intimate discussions took place between the Holy Three in that inner shrine of the eternal dwelling, as they contemplated the vast plan of redemption. Springing from their infinite love flowed out this purpose to reclaim members of a fallen race, to bring them to such high eternal destiny and glory: the means - the blood of the Lamb! That blood so precious because of the intrinsic worth of God incarnate, His sinless being 'without blemish'; and His unreproachable character, outwardly observable, 'without spot' (1 Pet.1:19). All divine purpose is bound up in the Lamb 'foreknown'.

Complementary to the truth of 1 Peter 1:20 is the remarkable reference in Revelation 13:8 to 'the Lamb that hath been slain from the foundation of the world': divine purpose spoken of as though already implemented! As Paul wrote in a different context: "God, who ... calleth the things that are not, as though they were" (Rom.4:17). It becomes clear that the creation of the world was effected by the Triune God in full knowledge that it would be marred by man's fall. Yet anticipating this, provision had already been made for the Lamb to be slain; a provision so early enshrined in the prophetic word to the serpent: "I will put enmity between thee and the woman, and between thy seed and her seed: it shall bruise thy head, and thou shalt bruise his heel" (Gen.3:15).

When in due time the Lamb had in fact been slain, the apostle Peter impressed on those who shared the guilt of their Messiah's crucifixion that this was by divine foreordination: "Him, being delivered up by the determinate counsel and foreknowledge of God, ye by the hand of lawless men did crucify and slay" (Acts 2:23).

Prefigurings

The figure of 'the Lamb' appears frequently in the divine record. Foreshadowings in narrative and ordinance abound. We hear the heart-searching enquiry from a loving son to his adoring father, "Behold, the fire and the wood: but where is the lamb for a burnt offering?" And Abraham's prophetic response: "God will provide himself the lamb for a burnt offering, my son" (Gen.22:7,8). Or again we envisage the unblemished male of the first year, fresh and vigorous, which was to be 'taken', 'kept' and 'killed' for the deliverance of the firstborn from God's judgement (Ex.12:21).

Would not the pathos felt in every family in Israel be felt also in the heart of Israel's God at this further preview of Calvary, where the Lamb of God would be slain? The sensitivity of the household 'slayer' would be high and real. The slaying of the lamb must nevertheless be carried out, stirring emotions which portrayed, however feebly, those which would move the heart of God when the Lamb was slain at Calvary.

The morning and evening lambs of the continual burnt offerings, with their meal and drink offerings, were a daily reminder to Israel of their need, so that the Lord would meet with them and dwell among them (Ex.29:39-41). Sin and trespass offerings likewise demanded the sacrificial lamb upon which human guilt and infringements of God's holy law were symbolically placed, by the laying of hands on the creature's head; forgiveness, purification and restoration were thereby obtained (see Lev.4 and Lev.14).

The Lamb Manifested and Slain

Aptly and willingly the Lord Jesus accepted the title of 'Lamb', which described the guilelessness and harmlessness of His character. The Sin-Bearer pointed out by the Baptist in Bethany beyond Jordan was the Messiah, God's Anointed One. Declared to be the Lamb of God at His baptism, John's followers, and indeed all the people of Israel, were given a clear indication of the Lord's true identity. However, for the most part 'they that were his own received him not', and His ultimate rejection ensued. Israel slew (literally violently laid hands upon) the Righteous One, and were pronounced guilty and accountable for the Saviour's death (Acts 5:30).

In Acts 10:39 a different word is used, meaning 'to take away, to cut off violently'. Yet all had been carried out in the determinate will and foreordained counsels of God, formulated and sanctioned by the Godhead (Acts 4:27,28). The Lord's silence before Caiaphas the high priest, and his co-conspirators, the chief priests, scribes and elders of the people ('the whole council') produced reactionary and inflammatory statements containing lies, insults, insinuations and accusations.

Pilate and Herod could not force Him to speak - He 'held his peace' (Matt.26:63); He 'answered nothing' (27:12). He 'no more answered anything' (Mk.15:5); He 'answered him nothing' (Lk.23:9).

Proceedings designed to 'catch Him out' totally failed. There had to be the fulfilment of Isaiah's words He 'opened not his mouth' (Is.53:7): no protest, no threat issued from those gracious lips. As the lamb of the sin offering (Lev.4) He would bear our griefs and woes, and in that experience would know the striking, smiting and affliction of God. He Himself was part of that triune counsel which decreed the slaying of the Lamb - 'smitten of God' (Elohim); He would alone bear the dreadful weight of our iniquity which the Lord (Jehovah) laid upon Him on the tree. Jeremiah, in a very similar way, was the gentle lamb led to the slaughter, but the difference from the Saviour was this: the divine Lamb was fully aware of all that awaited Him, whereas Jeremiah was unaware of his opponents' intentions (Jer.11:19). From the human standpoint we well understand the prophet's outburst: "But, O LORD of hosts ... let me see thy vengeance on them ..." (v.20). Contrast our Redeemer's pleading tones, "Father forgive ..."

The Lamb Exalted

Revelation 5 shares with us the apostle John's vision of a marvellous scene in heaven. The Lamb is seen in the midst of heaven's throne, surrounded by mighty angelic beings: "I saw ... a Lamb standing, as though it had been slain". Calvary can never be forgotten, its memory never erased, because the Lamb wears eternally the wounds of His sufferings sustained on earth. All heaven knew what John did not, that the Lamb alone was worthy to open the book and loose the seals. The twenty-eight beings nearest the throne prostrate themselves, singing a new song - that of the Lamb's atoning death and redeeming blood, and its world-wide effectuality. The crescendo gathers pace, uncountable numbers of the heavenly host accompanying the original worshippers to acclaim the Lamb.

Different choirs in heaven are featured at different times, all doubtless with the perfect pitch and harmony which must pervade those celestial spheres. Repeatedly in the Book of Revelation the loud symphonies of praise are heard. As when those who emerge victorious from the Great Tribulation holocaust unite to sing "the song of Moses the servant of God, and the song of the Lamb" (Rev.15:3). Of them we read that the caring Shepherd dries the tear-stained eyes with His nail-pierced hand, and gently guides His loved ones to fountains of waters of life (Rev.7:9-17). Precious identity of Shepherd and Lamb! At the Cross we view the exhaustless fount of God's mercy to the repentant. Those who oppose the overtures of grace will experience the fearful outpouring of the 'wrath of the Lamb', before which none can survive (Rev.6:16,17). Much later the eternal city comes into view (Rev.21). No temple is needed: the worship is direct and immediate. The God Almighty and the Lamb are present, giving light and glory. The throne is in the city, shared by Father and Son, never more to be separated. No curse, no night, no sin can ever find a place there. The Lamb foreknown in eternal past has made possible through His sacrifice the share of the redeemed in that future eternal day.

"Lamb of God, His Father's bosom

Ever was His dwelling-place;

His delight, in Him rejoicing,

One with Him in power and grace.

Oh, what wondrous love and mercy

Thus to lay His glory by,

And for us to come from heaven

As the Lamb of God to die!"

CHAPTER ELEVEN: THE CROSS FORETOLD – 'ALL THAT THE PROPHETS HAVE SPOKEN' (ALEX REID)

Generation after generation of believers have wondered what it would have been like to be on the Emmaus road and to have heard the Lord's exposition of "All that the prophets have spoken" concerning the sufferings of the Christ. No doubt if this had been possible many hearts would have shared the burning of heart with those favoured two. We are going to attempt, in this brief chapter, to examine some of the things that were written by Moses and the prophets, with specific fulfilment in the Cross of Christ and some of the events immediately associated with it. As we shall see, many of the things that took place during our Lord's passion were foretold centuries before they happened; some of them in the most remarkable detail.

To begin with, we turn to the book of Genesis, the book of beginnings. In Genesis 3:15, having confronted the disobedient man and woman with their transgression of His command, God turned to address the agent of their fall - the serpent. Through the serpent God is speaking to the malignant Evil One who has used the creature as his tool. God said, 'I will put enmity between you and the woman, and between your offspring and hers; he will crush your head and you will strike his heel'. The first part of the verse, if it stood on its own, could be interpreted as indicating only the continual conflict between good and evil as it is expressed in human history. But the words 'he' and 'you' in the second part of the verse indicate an occasion of conflict in which the Evil One would be defeated by a particular individual who, in overcoming him, would Himself experience pain.

Only one event in the sacred record fits the words of this prophecy. The writer to the Hebrews in 2:9,14 gives the Spirit-inspired answer to the Genesis prediction. He sees Jesus, a sharer in our humanity, true seed of the woman, experiencing death in order to destroy the Devil, the wielder of the power of death. In other words, he describes the experience of the Cross. Crucifixion was not a method of execution used by the Jews, whose means of inflicting capital punishment included for instance stoning to death (see Lev.20:2 etc.). It was a Gentile practice thought to have originated with the Phoenicians or Egyptians, to find a detailed description of it in the Psalms is surprising indeed. When David, in Psalm 22, describes the experience of a sufferer undergoing violence at the hands of enemies, he may not have had the act of crucifixion in mind, but such are the graphic details given, that they describe the experience of crucifixion. The fact that the Lord Jesus quoted the opening verse of this Psalm while hanging on the Cross (Matt.27:46; Mk.15:34) endorses its application to Himself as the Suffering One.

The original Hebrew of the opening verses of Psalm 22 is written in such a way as not always to give complete sentences, but a series of short ejaculations, which could be thought of as simulating the gasps or sobs of a dying man. One of the trials of death by crucifixion was that the victim, having his arms fixed to the cross member in an outstretched manner, was supporting his body-weight in an awkward way, making it difficult to breathe. So Psalm 22, which has been dubbed the psalm of sobs or sighs, seems in its very style of writing to be portraying the agony of crucifixion. A number of verses in Psalm 22 are suggestive of the physical trials of the Cross. For example, verse 14 depicts the stress on the human frame; verse 15 the dehydration and severe thirst of the victim; verse 16 the piercing of the hands and feet inflicted by the nails used to secure the sufferer. One commentator suggests the words of verse 17: 'I can count all my bones', could be interpreted 'I must display all my bones', thus indicating the humiliating nakedness of the victim. Added to this, other Old Testament passages bring clearly into focus the physical sufferings of the Christ; for example Isaiah 52:14 and Isaiah 53:3,5,10.

Along with the physical suffering predicted in Scripture goes a detailed description of the mental and psychological anguish experienced by Christ on the Cross. Psalm 69:1,2,14,15 likens the experience to that of a drowning man; the feeling of helplessness, of being over-whelmed and having none at hand to help. The mental suffering is heightened by feelings of humiliation and shame at being set at nought. The Lord's persecutors certainly tried to break His spirit with their sneers, words of scorn, reviling and humiliation (see Matt.27:39-44; Mk.15:29-32; Lk.23:35-37).

The keenness of this hurt is clearly brought before us in Psalm 22:6-8 and Psalm 69:7,14,20. His feeling of being set at nought, 'I am a worm and not a man', the insults, the mockery, the sarcasm are all here. The pain of such humiliation is all the more hurtful when it is palpably unjust (cf. Ps.69:4; Jn.15:25; Lk.23:4,13-15). Even His enemies and persecutors are described for us; strong bulls, roaring lions, dogs, are the manner in which they are described in the metaphoric language of Psalm 22, verses 12, 13, 16. The bulls and lions are those whose attacks are bold and ferocious and represent the most powerful and daring of His enemies, such as the Jewish leaders who brought the charges and the Roman soldiers who perpetrated the actual deed. The dogs are those who attack in packs in a cowardly way and would portray the mob that cried for Christ's blood and joined in the jeers and taunts.

Certain prophetic passages of Psalm 22 and Psalm 69 and Isaiah 53 are so amazingly accurate in their details that it is only when we see them fulfilled in the experience of Christ that we appreciate that they could not apply to anyone else but Him. Psalm 22 verse 18 predicts the dividing of His garments among His executioners, the perk of their grisly job, and of their casting lots for the seamless undergarment (see Matt.27:35; Mk.15:24). Psalm 69:21 foretells the offer of gall mixed with wine and myrrh (see Matt.27:34; Mk.15:23), a bitter concoction intended to dull the pain of execution; the verse also predicts the cruel jest of offering a man with raging thirst wine vinegar to drink (Matt.27:48; Mk.15:36; Lk.23:36; Jn.19:28-30). Isaiah 53:9 sets out the divine overruling in the burial arrangements immediately after the body was removed from the Cross.

"He was assigned a grave with the wicked and with the rich in his death". This somewhat cryptic statement is only decipherable when the facts are known about the intervention of the rich man, Joseph of Arimathea, in offering his own new tomb as an alternative to the communal grave that would normally have been assigned to criminals who had been executed together; for the Lord was crucified along with two criminals (see Matt.27:57-60; Mk.15:42-47; Lk.23:50-56; Jn.19:38-42).

Jeremiah in his lamentations, appealed to travellers passing by the city of Jerusalem; a city sacked, burned and devastated by the passage of the ruthless Babylonian army, to consider if the heart-rending scene before them had any meaning or message for them. "Is it nothing to you, all you who pass by? Look around and see. Is there any suffering like my suffering that was inflicted on me, that the LORD brought on me in the day of his fierce anger?" (Lam.1:12). The prophet makes his appeal all the more poignant by taking the personal pronouns 'my' and 'me' and applying them to the dying city. Throughout the Christian era, earnest readers of Scripture have heard in these words the appeal of the Cross of Christ to their own souls. What has been our response as we have considered those sufferings together?

(Biblical quotations are from the NIV)

CHAPTER TWELVE: THE CROSS FORETOLD – 'IN ALL THE SCRIPTURES' (ALEX JARVIS)

It is fascinating to speculate which scriptures our Lord referred to during the seven-mile journey to Emmaus. Did He go through the Old Testament chronologically? Or did He trace His journey to Calvary step-by-step using non-sequential Scriptural references? For this chapter, I have taken the latter approach. Perhaps Jesus began with the very first verse of Genesis 1, "In the beginning God created the heaven and the earth", knowing that some decades later, the disciple whom He loved would begin his gospel narrative with similar words: "In the beginning was the Word, and the Word was with God, and the Word was God ... All things were made by him; and without him was not anything made that hath been made" (Jn.1:1,3).

Thus the Co-creator prepared for creation. But what happened between the first two verses of Genesis 1? Did our Lord make a creation that was 'waste and void'? This seems to me unlikely in the light of Isaiah 45:18: 'God; that formed the earth and made it; he established it, he created it not a waste'. So what cataclysmic happening caused the creation to be turned into a waste? Our Lord told His disciples: 'I beheld Satan fallen like lightning from heaven' (Lk.10:18). Could it be that the entry of sin into heaven itself – as Satan attempted to usurp God's throne - was the event which triggered the voiding of God's first creation? For how many millennia the earth remained in darkness, we are not told: the divine calendar is silent. But one day, as eternity unfolded, "the Spirit of God moved upon the face of the waters"; and Father, Son and Spirit in perfect harmony began their work of creation for a second time. Thus one can imagine our Lord explaining to His companions the origin of sin. *(Editors' note: This interpretation of the creation narratives has been advanced by some expositors; alternative interpretations are of course advanced by others).*

This second creation culminated - on the sixth day - in another scripture He may have quoted: "Let us make man in our image, after our likeness" (Gen.1:26). The first Adam was made in sinless perfection, modelled on the divine Being. Yet no sooner was he placed in Eden, than Satan began his relentless work of revenge, determined to mar God's perfect creation.

The period of time which elapsed between Adam's creation and his fall: was it simply a matter of days? Or did God come down in the cool of the day to walk with Adam and Eve beneath Eden's trees for several months, or even years? Again, Scripture is silent; but one thing we can be sure of is that on each and every occasion Satan watched, poised to strike. And seated on heaven's throne another Watcher waited, knowing that the entry of sin, 'and death through sin' would trigger a sequence of events that would inexorably lead to Calvary. The first Adam, confronted and tempted by sin, fell. Satan triumphed. The divine plan of salvation, formed 'before the foundation of the world', then came into play. The second Adam, although assailed by sin on every hand, and tempted at every turn, never succumbed; He remained sinless. Satan's temptations failed.

Having explained to His fellow travellers how sin had entered the world - 'and death through sin' – and the consequential need for a redemptive sacrifice, one can imagine the Lord unfolding from Scripture the type of sacrifice that needed to be offered. He referred perhaps to Genesis 4: "And the Lord had respect unto Abel and to his offering: but unto Cain and to his offering he had not respect" (v.4,5). Why did God not accept Cain's sacrifice? He had, after all, put a lot of effort into growing his crops. Tilling the ground, in the sweat of his brow, was arguably more onerous than looking after a few sheep! Yet it was *not* accepted, whilst Abel's was. This was because there had been no shedding of blood. There was nothing in the offering of Cain's fruit and vegetables to speak to the Father of the wondrous sacrifice of His beloved and only begotten Son.

It is unthinkable that our righteous God would not have explained to *both* brothers the need for, and significance of, the shedding of blood in the offerings that were required. Abel obeyed; Cain did his own thing, thinking his ideas were better. How often do we act like Cain? Knowing best; ignoring God's Word; following our own inclinations! It is probable that the Lord would also have included Exodus 12 among the Scriptures that He "interpreted ... concerning himself": "... when I see the blood, I will pass over you" (v.13), would have been a key phrase, well known to these two disciples, as to all Jews; and pivotal to their faith.

'With desire, I have desired to eat this Passover with you before I suffer' (Lk.22:15), He could say to His disciples. And so He made careful arrangements to ensure a suitable (upper) room was available for the occasion. The Lord wanted privacy for this feast: it was the last that He would keep under the Old Covenant and He alone uniquely knew that His hour had come. The Passover was about to become redundant: "For our Passover also hath been sacrificed, even Christ" (1 Cor.5:7). So He might have explained to His two enthralled companions the significance of the careful instructions which Moses had given so many centuries earlier, to enable His people then to find shelter beneath the blood of those lambs slain in Goshen. In just the same way, the Lord Jesus gave considerate forethought and careful instructions for the keeping of the Remembrance - the Passover's New Covenant replacement - which is equally pivotal to our faith today. "This do in remembrance of me". How *could* we forget? Yet we do; and, knowing that we would, He made loving provision for us, despite the fearsome, looming prospect of Calvary.

Having set the scene for the need for redemption to be gained through "the blood of a lamb without blemish and without spot", our Lord may well have referred next to Abraham: "And Abraham took the wood of the burnt offering, and laid it upon Isaac his son" (Gen.22:6). How poignant a reminder of the time when He went out from Pilate's final judgement bearing the cross for himself. Weighed down by that rough-hewn baulk of timber; and picturing Isaac with the kindling wood strapped to his back. Both advancing to the place of sacrifice. As the Saviour drew the parallel between Isaac and Himself, it was there that the resemblance ended. For Jesus there was no ram caught in the thicket; no voice from heaven to stay the hand wielding the sword of judgement. As the hymn writer so aptly puts it: *That fearful stroke, it fell on Him, And life for us was won.*

Abraham told Isaac: "God will provide himself the lamb for a burnt offering" (Gen.22:8); and now centuries later, the prophecy was fulfilled when "once at the end of the ages" Christ has "been manifested to put away sin by the sacrifice of himself" (Heb.9:26). So, gently and lovingly, the Lord brings His listeners to the manner of His death, perhaps illustrating the explanation from the incident recorded by Moses: "... and it came to pass, that if a serpent had bitten any man, when he looked unto the serpent of brass, he lived" (Num.26:9). Had His audience heard from some of their fellow-disciples of the conversation Jesus had held with Nicodemus a few years earlier?

Then, He had explained that "as Moses lifted up the serpent in the wilderness, even so must the Son of man be lifted up" (Jn.3:14). Thus one may imagine the Lord explaining the events leading up to the moment when he "bore our sins in his body upon the tree". As the little group of travellers drew near to the outskirts of Emmaus, Jesus drew His narrative to a close. Maybe He referred - as He had to the scribes and Pharisees on an earlier occasion - to Jonah: "as Jonah was three days and three nights in the belly of the whale; so shall the Son of man be three days and three nights in the heart of the earth" (Matt.12:40). Jesus may also have reminded His companions of the words of David: "For thou wilt not leave my soul in Sheol; neither wilt thou suffer thine holy one to see corruption" (Ps.16:10). The rumours which had been circulating in Jerusalem, and which Cleopas had relayed to the Lord, were evidently true, as Jesus explained from these Scriptures: it was now the third day and the Christ was *indeed* risen from the dead.

We can almost hear Jesus repeating to His companions the angel's question: "Why seek ye the living among the dead? He ... is risen" (Lk.24:5,6). Moments later they reached their home and invited their fellow-traveller to come in for a meal. And there, around that simple supper table, as He broke bread, they saw with amazement the nail-prints in His hands. This was no stranger! He was their beloved Master. Risen indeed! Gloriously alive. Like those other disciples at the tomb, they too remembered His words. Sadly, there are many today for whom these words have no meaning; and for whom the Lord is not risen and glorified. Their eyes are blinded to His true identity by Satan, who is succeeding in his attempts to blind "the minds of the unbelieving" (2 Cor.4:4). But we can rejoice with those two dear disciples who - their tiredness and despondency forgotten - raced back to Jerusalem to relay to the eleven "the things that happened in the way, and how he was known of them in the breaking of the bread" (Lk.24:35).

CHAPTER THIRTEEN: THE CROSS FORETOLD – 'NOW IS MY SOUL TROUBLED' (JOHN ARCHIBALD)

The Lord Jesus spoke of the circumstances of His death on a number of occasions during His public ministry on earth. We know this from the Gospel writers in the Scriptures. An important example is the conversation at Caesarea Philippi in Matthew 16:13- 23, where the Lord asked His disciples, "'Who say ye that I am?" Peter replied, "Thou art the Christ, the Son of the living God'". There follows the Lord's wonderful revelation about the Church which is His Body and then we read, "From that time began Jesus to shew unto his disciples, how that he must go unto Jerusalem, and suffer many things of the elders and chief priests and scribes, and be killed, and the third day be raised up" (v.21). It seems that although there are earlier allusions to His death, such as John 3:14-16, it was not until this confession by Peter and the Lord's announcement, "I will build my church", that He began to describe more specifically where and how and at whose hands He would die.

When the disciples acknowledged Him as the Christ, He began to unveil the mystery of the Christ (the expression later used by Paul to describe the Church the Body in Ephesians 3:4), and only then did He begin to give details of how the leaders of Israel would ill-treat the Messiah, and of the sacrifice that would make possible the building of such an impregnable Church. Peter reacted strongly against the Lord's words about His suffering and death, which brought from the Lord the counter rebuke "Get thee behind me, Satan: thou art a stumbling block unto me" (v.23). It is very sobering to reflect that Satan could speak through one of the Lord's apostles, when Peter put his own desires and inclinations ahead of the will of God and the word of the Lord. We should take heed. There is also an indication here of the Adversary's opposition to the purposes of God in the Cross.

Later, as the Lord and His disciples were on the final journey to Jerusalem, we read in Matthew 20:17-20 that He took the twelve apostles aside and told them again what the leaders of Israel would do to Him, and supplied added information about the Gentile involvement in mocking, scourging and crucifying Him. This seems to be the first completely explicit reference to crucifixion as the manner of His own death, although in Matthew 16 He did invite those who would follow Him to take up their own crosses. These utterances of the Lord in Matthew 16 and Matthew 20 give factual detail about how He was to die. We turn now to scriptures which give some indication of how He and His Father God viewed this prospect.

Beloved and Chosen (Lk.9:28-36)

About eight days after the conversation of Matthew 16 at Caesarea Philippi, the Lord took Peter, John and James up into a high mountain and was transfigured before them, so that His face shone as the sun and His garments became white as the light. Luke tells us that Jesus was speaking to His Father when this transformation took place. There followed a conversation with Moses and Elijah, who appeared in glory and spoke of "his decease which He was about to accomplish at Jerusalem". Finally, a voice from God was heard, proclaiming Jesus to be God's beloved Son in whom He was well pleased, and that He was God's chosen. In this way God the Father ascribed honour and glory to His beloved Son (2 Pet.1:17), and declared His complete satisfaction with the One whom He had chosen for the sacrifice which had been the subject of discussion on the holy mount.

We believe this is referred to in Hebrews 2:9, "Jesus ... crowned with glory and honour, that by the grace of God he should taste death for every man". This glorious experience of the three amazed apostles became for them a wonderful confirmation of the accord between the Father and the Son about the death of the Cross. They were commanded to tell no man until after the resurrection, just as the disciples were charged at Caesarea Philippi to tell no man that Jesus was the Christ.

Constrained and Compelled (Lk.12:50)

Here the Lord speaks of His death as a baptism. He must go down beneath the deep, dark waters of divine judgement and of death. As He contemplates this He says, "How am I straitened till it be accomplished'. The Greek word translated 'straitened' (RV) or 'distressed' (NIV) has the thought of someone under pressure or constraint resulting in confinement to a certain course of action. What were those pressures in His case? One pressure was the determined purpose of the Godhead that the Son should be sacrificed on Calvary. From this the Son would never deviate. Another was the deep revulsion of God the Son against sin and its consequence - the death of the Cross, which meant that God would make Him "who knew no sin to be sin on our behalf" (2 Cor.5:21). Yet another was the prospect of incurring the ancient curse of God on "every one that hangeth on a tree" (Gal.3:13).

These pressures were in addition to His deep awareness of the acute shame and physical suffering that such a death would involve. As the inevitable day of this awful experience drew nearer, the Lord approached it with unwavering resolve, compelled by His devotion to His Father and His love for the lost, but this statement indicates the enormous burden that He felt. Is it not a source of continuing amazement for us that the One who reigns supreme and whose power none can withstand, was prepared to endure such constraint?

'Now is my soul troubled' (Jn.12:24-33)

The pressure of this burden is evident again as the Lord speaks of the need for the grain of wheat to fall into the earth and die if there is to be any harvest. As the RV margin suggests, we should read "Father save me from this hour" (v.27) with a question mark as part of the Lord's question: "Now is my soul troubled and what shall I say?" He could not make an unqualified request to His Father to save Him from this, because it was the divine will that He should endure it. We note also that on this occasion when He signifies by what manner of death He should die. He refers also to the defeat of the Adversary that will result from it, and to the universal consequences to mankind of His sacrifice.

All men will be drawn to Him, either in salvation or for judgement. We must not fail to receive the Lord's challenge as He discusses the immense implications of His own fulfilment of His Father's will. "If any man serve me, let Him follow me ... him will the Father honour" (v.26). What an example we have to follow!

Chosen and Rejected (Matt.21:33-46)

This parable of the vineyard seems to have been given in the last week before Calvary, and it graphically portrays the response of the leaders of Israel to the sending of God's Son. "They took him and cast him forth out of the vineyard, and killed him". The One who was chosen and precious with God was rejected by those who were His own people. "The stone which the builders rejected, the same was made the head of the comer" (v.42). Peter repeats this quotation from Psalm 118 in the second chapter of his first epistle, where he explains the precious teaching of the house of God, the people of God and the holy nation. 1 Peter 2:8 identifies the nation to whom the kingdom of God was to be given after it was taken from Israel. In view of this repeated use of Psalm 118:22 in discussion of the house of God and people of God in New Testament times, must we not draw the lesson that any inclination to minimize the importance of God's pattern of collective service contains an element of rejection of the Lord as 'head of the corner'? Undoubtedly one of the Lord's great sorrows as He approached the Cross was His keen sense of rejection by those who were His own.

Troubled and Betrayed (Jn.13:21)

As the Lord sat with His apostles in the Upper Room on the night before He went to the Cross, an additional sorrow troubled His spirit. One of His own apostles would betray Him. If Paul received his information about the Lord's supper directly from the Lord, as seems indicated by 1 Corinthians 11:23, then we would also deduce from that verse that in speaking to Paul, the Lord described the night before His death as 'the night in which I was betrayed'. The betrayal was so much upon His mind that He used it to identify a night in which so much else took place.

Later that evening the Lord referred to Judas in His prayer for the disciples. "While I was with them, I kept them ... and I guarded them, and not one of them perished, but the son of perdition" (Jn.17:12). The loss of Juda may have troubled the Lord as much as the consequences of betrayal. Of Judas we read that he fell away from his place in ministry and apostleship "that he might go to his own place" (Acts 1:25). Despite his close acquaintance with the Lord, Judas chose eternal darkness and loss and it was a sore grief to Christ. The Lord went to the Cross with a deep care and concern for the lost, and a sad heart for all those who would refuse to believe in Him.

Prospect of Delight (Heb.12:2)

Before leaving this solemn subject we must mention a further prospect which gave great delight to the Lord as He approached the Cross. In Matthew 13:44 we find the parable of the treasure hidden in the field. It is written of the man who found the treasure that "in his joy he goeth and selleth all that he hath, and buyeth that field". We understand that the man of the parable is the Lord Himself, and the joy is the joy that was set before Him, for which He endured the Cross and despised the shame. Our Lord 'sold all that He had' in order to purchase the treasure for Himself, and wonder of wonders, He did it joyfully.

As we read the Gospel narratives which portray so vividly the words and attitude of Christ as He made His lonely and sorrowful way to the Cross, we can surely discern His unshakable determination and His glad eagerness to give Himself, in order to secure the fruit and the treasure and the delight of His God and Father.

CHAPTER FOURTEEN: THE CROSS - CRUCIFIED IN WEAKNESS (MICHAEL ELLIOTT)

The Mind of Christ

As we approach our subject it is helpful to remind ourselves of Paul's teaching in Philippians 2 regarding Christ's attitude to the tremendous stoop He made in leaving heaven and coming to serve here on earth. Paul tells us that although Christ was one with God yet He made Himself of no reputation taking the form of a bondservant (v.7). As we look at our subject we see that this involved His humbling of Himself and becoming "obedient to the point of death, even the death of the cross" (v.8). This act of humbling was a voluntary one by Christ just as His death on the Cross was one of voluntary obedience. Although our chapter is titled 'Crucified in Weakness' it is important to recognize all took place because it was in accordance with "the determined counsel and foreknowledge of God" (Acts 2:23).

It was not the physical pain and suffering of Christ that caused His death on the Cross. His death was due to His obedience, an act of His will when, having completed everything the Father had required of Him in relation to dealing with sin. He could say, "Father, into Your hands I commend My spirit" (Lk.23:46).

Gethsemane

On leaving the Upper Room the Lord came to the Mount of Olives and then to the place called Gethsemane (Matt.26:30,36).

We note in passing its name means 'oil press'. It was a place the Lord and His disciples visited frequently. Indeed, Luke tells us the Lord often spent whole nights there and so, no doubt, the disciples also when they had nowhere else to sleep (Lk.21:37; 22:39). Not unnaturally, Judas was also familiar with the arrangement (Jn.18:2).

We have no way of telling how many times the Lord came to the Garden either with His disciples or alone, but surely each time would serve as a reminder of what lay before Him. It is remarkable yet understandable that the Lord should wish others to share in His grief. Of course the disciples could never carry the burden the Lord was uniquely to bear at Calvary, but it was His heartfelt desire that Peter, James and John, especially, should watch with Him whilst He "began to be sorrowful and deeply distressed" (Matt.26:37,38).

We know they were so tired and confused by the whole situation they were unable even to share in this aspect of the Lord's suffering. How true, 'The spirit indeed is willing, but the flesh is weak' (Matt.26:41). Yet this was not a word of rebuke. He just longed that they might watch and pray with Him whilst He, a stone's throw from them, prostrated Himself in prayer before God. Luke tells us of an angel being sent from heaven to strengthen the Lord (22:43). It is from Luke also we learn that the Lord's agony of soul and spirit resulted in His sweat becoming like great drops of blood falling down to the ground (22:44). It is no doubt in the Spirit's overruling that the Lord's prayers have been so briefly summarized, but what has been recorded must surely move our hearts deeply. He addressed God as 'Abba, Father', an expression both of deep trust and intimacy, the essence of His prayer being, "All things are possible for You. Take this cup away from Me; nevertheless, not what I will, but what You will" (Mk.14:36).

Three times the Lord's prayer came up to His God and each time the prayer contained the heartfelt words "nevertheless, not as I will, but as You will". The writer of the Hebrews tells us a little more for he says they were offered up with "vehement cries and tears" and then that the Lord "was heard because of His godly fear". Thus the divine comment is that Christ learned obedience (that is, the cost of obedience) by the things which He suffered (Heb.5:7,8).

As the Lord rose from prayer Judas and the armed band came to the Garden to arrest Him. Judas came with the authority of the chief priests and elders of the people and brought with him a great multitude, including temple guards (Lk.22:52) and Roman soldiers (Jn.18:3). They were armed with swords and clubs, as though to arrest a criminal. When Jesus saw them He asked the question, "Whom are you seeking?" to which they responded, "Jesus of Nazareth". It is John alone who tells us that when the Lord replied with the words, "I am He" that the crowd drew back and fell to the ground, as they surely must in the presence of Deity (Jn.18:4-6).

The Lord had the power and authority to resist arrest, and He could have called on His Father to send more than twelve legions of angels (Matt.26:53), but His desire was to please His Father. Peter would strike out to protect his Lord. The Lord, alone, willingly went with them, knowing all that lay before Him, taking time despite His own grief to show compassion in the healing of Malchus (Lk.22:50,51).

The Lord's Trials - Before the Sanhedrin

Immediately after His arrest the Lord was bound and brought before Annas, father-in-law of Caiaphas (Jn.18:12-15), prior to appearing before the representatives of the Sanhedrin which had been hurriedly assembled to meet during the night hours. They needed to find a legal basis on which to condemn Him to death and so various witnesses were sought who might speak against Him. Matthew tells us of many false witnesses coming forward, but to all the charges Jesus remained silent (Matt.26:59-63). Caiaphas became desperate in his attempts to find a charge against the Lord and putting Him under oath commanded, "Tell us if You are the Christ, the Son of God!' To this Jesus replied: "It is as you said ..." (Matt.26:63,64). We can only wonder at the hardness of their hearts for in response to the Lord's reply Caiaphas tore his clothes, accusing the Lord of speaking blasphemy and condemning Him to death.

Likewise we can only wonder at the Lord's grace for Matthew tells us, "They then spat in His face and beat Him; and others struck Him with the palms of their hands, saying, 'Prophesy to us, Christ! Who is the one who struck You'" (Matt.26:67,68). He did know who was doing these things and one day they will be called to give account for their terrible words and deeds. Now as morning came the Sanhedrin formally came together to condemn the Lord and hand Him over to Pilate to carry out the death sentence (Jn.18:31,32).

The Lord's Trials – Before Pilate and Herod

John tells us it was in the early morning Jesus was led from Caiaphas to the Praetorium (Jn.18:28). Ironically the Jews did not go in to the Praetorium in case they should defile themselves and thus not be able to eat the Passover. The Lord was to be examined by Pilate (Jn.18:28-19:16), and by Herod (Lk.23:6-12) when Pilate realized the Lord was a Galilean. It is sad to note that a friendship developed between the two men on the basis of their evil dealings with the Lord. At the point at which the Lord was brought before Pilate the first time He had already suffered many hours of shame and suffering at the hands of the Sanhedrin. Now the Jews sought to have Pilate find the Lord guilty of treason on the basis that He said He was the King of the Jews. Both Pilate and Herod were responsible for the Lord being mocked and physically abused.

Luke records, "Then Herod, with his men of war, treated Him with contempt and mocked Him, arrayed Him in a gorgeous robe, and sent Him back to Pilate" (Lk.23:11). The Prince of Peace was thus treated by men of war. For his part Pilate tried every ploy available to him to release One whom he recognized to be an innocent Man, but the people were insistent that Barabbas not the Lord should be set free.

Even after Pilate took Jesus and scourged Him and in mockery dressed Him as a king in a purple robe, and with a crown of twisted thorns upon His head and a reed in His right hand, the people were vehement in their words, "... If you let this Man go, you are not Caesar's friend" (Jn.19:12). Finally Pilate sat down at the place of judgement, The Pavement or Gabbatha, and for one last time presented the Messiah to His people, "Behold your King" (Jn.19:14). Their response has rung down the centuries, "Away with Him, away with Him! Crucify Him" (Jn.19:15).

Golgotha

How poignantly John writes about the Lord's way to Golgotha, "And He, bearing His cross, went out to a place called the Place of a Skull, which is called in Hebrew, Golgotha, where they crucified Him ..." (Jn.19:17,18). Elsewhere we read of Simon of Cyrene being compelled to share the weight of the cross-beam with the Lord (Matt.27:32). Physically and mentally drained He now came to the place of sacrifice. We close by challenging ourselves with the words of the apostle Peter, "For to this you were called, because Christ also suffered for us, leaving us an example, that you should follow His steps: 'Who committed no sin, nor was guile found in His mouth', who, when He was reviled, did not revile in return; when He suffered, He did not threaten, but committed Himself to Him who judges righteously" (1 Pet.2:21-23).

(Biblical quotations from the NKJV)

CHAPTER ONE: BLESSED ARE THE POOR IN SPIRIT (GILBERT GRIERSON)

How wonderful that our God should want to bless His creatures! In Genesis 1:28 God blessed the man and the woman that He had formed in His own image. He has not changed in His desires because, as the apostle John reminds us, "God is love" (1). To bestow blessings on the earth and on its inhabitants was in the divine plan for mankind from the beginning. "The blessing of the Lord makes rich, and he adds no sorrow with it" (2). How sad that so much blessing was lost when Adam sinned. Adam's fallen race has been afflicted with the consequences of one man's disobedience from that day until this (3). But thank God that another Man has appeared to put things right and to restore the blessings of heaven.

In Matthew chapter 5 we have what is sometimes called 'The Sermon on the Mount', beginning with the 'beatitudes', meaning 'blessings'. The Greek word translated 'blessed' means to be fortunate, well off, counted happy. It was a happy day when great multitudes came together to listen to life-giving words from the mouth of God incarnate. Perhaps some were only there that day for the hoped-for physical blessings: healing of bodies and minds and perhaps another miraculously provided meal of bread and fishes. But that day the table was being set with food of a spiritual nature, food that is still available!

But what was the nature of the blessings that Jesus spoke about? Come with me please on a journey. Our destination is Bethlehem. Here we are in Manger Square, and in front of the Church of the Nativity, reputedly built over the birthplace of Israel's Messiah. Let's enter! Its low, isn't it? Mind your head! This door, the only entrance into the cavernous interior, is called the Door of Humility, so-called because everyone who wants to enter needs to bend low. The medieval crusader or the proud conqueror will not ride mounted in here; and even the common tourist has to bend!

And that serves as an illustration for this, the first of the beatitudes. It indicates that the way to experience the blessings of the kingdom is reserved not for everyone, but for those who are 'poor in spirit'. The same characteristics of the persons these blessings are offered to are clearly described by God in the words of the prophet Isaiah: "But this is the one to whom I will look: He who is humble and contrite in spirit and trembles at my word" (4).

These are the poor in spirit. Biblical history could fill a gallery with their portraits, men and women who deeply felt their own unworthiness before a holy God. Let's stop for a moment in front of Peter's portrait. Here he is out fishing on a boat on Galilee (5). He has fished all night with his companions and caught nothing. Now Jesus instructs him to cast his net on the other side. Sceptical, but willing to obey, Peter lowers the net. Now look at the huge catch that almost breaks the net! Wait, Peter is getting down at the feet of the Lord Jesus, recognising that he is in the presence of holiness, of deity. He confesses, "Depart from me, for I am a sinful man, O Lord." (6). He is indeed a sinful man, always was, but now he recognises it, as someone convicted by the Spirit of God, and so qualified to be blessed by the God he is beginning to know personally. This incident and others, especially when he denied the Lord three times, would always, throughout Peter's life as a disciple of the Lord Jesus, be a reality check as to the nature of the pit from which he had been lifted (7) to be the recipient of the divine blessings for which he was so totally unworthy.

Only the King of Heaven could speak with authority about the 'kingdom of heaven'. The values of this new kingdom are indeed upside down, for it is the convicted who are converted, those who die who live, those who weep who laugh, those who mourn who dance, those who are first torn who are graciously made whole, and those who are poor who are rich!

Bible quotations from the ESV: (1) 1 Jn.4:8 (2) Prov.10:22 (3) Rom.5:19 (4) Is.66:2 (5) Lk.5 (6) verse 8 (7) Is.38:17

CHAPTER TWO: BLESSED ARE THOSE WHO MOURN (ANDREW DORRICOTT)

As I sit down to explore this scripture and better understand the depth and breadth of its fuller meaning, it is impossible for me not to reflect on my own experiences of mourning. I realize that over four years have gone by since my wife's and my first child, a precious little girl born far too early, passed away despite weeks of pleading with God to heal her sick little heart. You might have your own experiences that this verse brings to the forefront of your mind. I can still feel the shortness of breath in between tears, and I can remember when I felt as though I had no more tears left. As strong as those memories are, they are but symptoms of a deeper mourning. And while God has been so gentle and gracious in granting much healing of my heart, I still mourn for Jadyn, and probably always will.

At the tomb of Lazarus, amidst a sea of people weeping and mourning his loss, it says of the Lord that "He groaned in the spirit and was troubled" (1). There is of course the famous verse, "Jesus wept" (2) at the very same scene. His weeping was the symptom, or the release, of the deep emotions He was feeling. But His emotions were even more than what the people around Him were experiencing. This is not the way God had intended it to be when He created the world and all that is in it. He had designed a paradise for His creation to enjoy, and people to worship Him and have communion with Him. But before long sin entered that paradise and destroyed it. This perfect world had fallen so far, sin had engulfed all that was in it, and death the result of sin (3), was and is now, an everyday occurrence in life.

The Lord Jesus Christ was there in the beginning with God the Father, and intricately involved in the creation, "... and without Him nothing was made that was made" (4). He was also acutely aware of what was His purpose for being on the earth: to bear the punishment for all sin. His reaction was more than for Lazarus, it was for the effects of sin and death on His beloved creation which resulted in such sadness and weeping and mourning.

Do you mourn over your sin? Do you mourn over the sins of others, those whom you know, and even those whom you don't? This is the heart of a repentant person, one who is aware of their condition before God. It is the only way to salvation, the genuine confessing of sin and true repentance to God through the saving work of Christ Jesus (5). But it doesn't end there, the longer we are believers, the more aware we become of the sin in our lives and how we continue to fail and "fall short of the glory of God" (6). We realize more and more how destitute and helpless we are. Our sadness is a deep mourning, mourning that will not go away or fade over time. Our response to mourning is so aptly described by David, "Oh, that I had the wings of a dove! I would fly away and be at rest - I would flee far away and stay in the desert; I would hurry to my place of shelter, far from the tempest and storm" (7).

Where is our comfort? Where is the happiness for the sad? Simply, yet profoundly, it is in the life-giving salvation through Jesus Christ. As we grow more aware of our sin, and as our mourning intensifies, we are able to even further appreciate the salvation of our Lord, how He bore the punishment for our sins and has freed us from bondage to sin. We have the sure hope of eternity spent with Him, sealed by the giving of the Holy Spirit, who is also called the comforter and lives in our hearts.

We are expected to mourn, truly mourn, for our sins and for the sins of this world. In doing so, we will invariably find ourselves in awe, in worship, in praise and in comfort of the blessings that Christ has made available to us through His ultimate sacrifice. Looking forward to eternity with Him, yes; but we can enjoy the sweetness of His comfort even now knowing that we have been completely forgiven. "If we confess our sins, he is faithful and just and will forgive us our sins and purify us from all unrighteousness" (8). Happy are the sad, for they will be comforted.

Bible quotations from the NKJV unless otherwise stated: (1) Jn.11:33 (2) Jn.11:35 (3) Rom.6:23 (4) Jn.1:3 (5) Rom.10:9 (6) Rom.3:23 (7) Ps.55:6-8 NIV (8) 1 Jn.1:9 NIV

CHAPTER THREE: BLESSED ARE THOSE WHO ARE GENTLE (ANDY SEDDON)

Meekness means gentleness, mildness and humility; hardly the qualities you imagine being promoted in first century Israel under the might of the Romans! What about our own 21st century, competitive culture? Don't we have to shout to be heard? Don't we have to jump to be seen? Don't we have to fight to get what we want? One of the 2011 contestants in BBC television's 'The Apprentice' boasted to the cameras "I am cold and hard ... I am unstoppable"; is this the necessary attitude to be successful in life? According to Jesus, no! He had a different view of success: not getting power or money, but becoming like Him by being kind, gentle and loving.

The Gentle Christ

Many Jews were excited about Jesus. They thought He would be a powerful military king who would defeat the Roman occupiers and re-establish Israel as a leading nation. Surely these people were confused when they heard Him speak and observed Him at work. Jesus said, "I am gentle and lowly in heart" (1). If we take His yoke upon us we will find rest for our souls. In a world of restlessness, it is the Lord's quiet, gentle nature that brings peace to those who follow. Isaiah's prophecy was fulfilled in Jesus: "He will not cry aloud or lift up his voice ... a bruised reed he will not break ..." (2).

Perhaps the most vivid picture of the Lord's meekness was when He made His entry into Jerusalem, after the manner foretold by the prophet Zechariah: "Behold, your king is coming to you ... humble and mounted on a donkey, on a colt, the foal of a donkey" (3). The New Testament is full of examples of how the Lord was gentle; with His disciples, with His family, with the sinner, with the poor and with His accusers.

The Power of Gentleness

Jesus said that the gentle (or the meek) would "inherit the earth" (4). Perhaps it is helpful at this point to remember who the earth belongs to in the first place. David writes: "the earth is the LORD'S, and everything in it" (5). We read elsewhere that the evil one currently has control over the world, but it is those who follow the owner who will inherit it, not those who follow the imposter. To 'inherit' therefore must mean to somehow share ownership of it, of its situations, of its people, and we are not just talking about future times, but now.

Do not our own experiences as well as the Scriptures show us that gentleness achieves what our natural ill temper, impatience and throwing our weight around does not? These victories can be in our relationships, our gospel witness, our employment and our Christian service. For example, a "gentle answer turns away wrath" (6) and therefore the gentle are able to keep the peace in contentious situations.

Paul demonstrated gentleness in his leadership over God's people, even when rebuke and discipline were necessary (7). He thereby won over people for the greater cause. This is a lesson for anybody in similar positions, whether it is youth leaders, overseers, or those with managerial responsibilities at work. Gentleness when we are sharing the gospel (without compromising the truth, of course) will more likely gain us listening ears. Learning to listen before we speak will help us better understand our peers (8). Acts of kindness rather than revenge will win over even our enemies (9). All these and more are examples of a gentle character.

It should be stressed that being gentle does not mean being weak, soft or easily influenced. Christ was certainly not like this and we are not called to be. However, in a world of human and consumer rights, it can feel infuriating when we do not receive from others what we think we deserve. The sinful nature wants to fight and selfishly complain. At such times it is helpful to remember that we are God's own people in God's own world. We don't have to fight for anything! 'His divine power has granted to us all things that pertain to life and godliness' (10). It is for this reason that we, like Jesus, can entrust ourselves to "him who judges justly" (11)

Bible quotations from the ESV, unless otherwise stated: (1) Matt.11:29 (2) Is.42:2-3; cf. Matt.12:19-20 (3) Zech.9:9 (4) Matt.5:5 (5) Ps.24:1 NIV (6) Prov.15:1 NIV (7) 1 Thess.2:7; 1 Tim.3:3 (8) Jas.1:19 (9) Rom.12:19-20 (10) 2 Pet.1:3 (11) 1 Pet.2:23

CHAPTER FOUR: BLESSED ARE THOSE WHO HUNGER AND THIRST FOR RIGHTEOUSNESS (RICHARD HUTCHINSON)

This chapter deals with yet another sort of person largely overlooked in secular society, but valued in Christ's manifesto for His kingdom, the Sermon on the Mount: those who hunger and thirst for righteousness. A determination to do right and see right being done cannot be a successful tactic in the aggrandizement of one's lot. The world sides more readily with those whose morals follow the relativist's motto: "There is no right or wrong, save that which you decide for yourself." The Lord's promise to those gathered with Him on the mountainside, however, was that those who hunger and thirst for righteousness will be satisfied. What can we take from that? First, we should get a handle on what exactly the hunger and thirst is for. Righteousness means 'self-evidently right and just', an absolute value, one with no grey areas, but perfect in and of itself. It is therefore, necessarily, of God.

In what way might one hunger and thirst for such a thing? Two examples present themselves. Firstly, we can desire to see the righteousness of God at work in the world around us, where we see so much inequity and that desire shall certainly be satisfied when the kingdom of God becomes a physical reality with Christ's return to rule and sit as judge over the nations. More pertinently, though, we can long for the revelation of God's righteousness within ourselves, aware of how far we are from exhibiting it in our lives. In the second case there is a much more present application - there has to be with each Beatitude given that "Blessed are" is present tense, implying a contentment in each instance in the here-and-now - because we can experience a genuine sense of God's righteousness in our lives today. Indeed, this should be a hallmark of the spiritual kingdom of God today (1).

How so? We must first acknowledge the Cross in this work before all else because "for our sake He made Him to be sin who knew no sin, so that in Him we might become the righteousness of God" (2). The Lord Jesus, who was perfectly righteous, took our sin, so that we might take His righteousness in its place. We would have no chance at satisfaction without that, no matter how we hungered or thirsted, and through Christ's death there is a righteousness that is ours already in an eternal sense. That is secure and, when all is said and done, it is that righteousness that God will recognise as our right to be in His presence, both in meetings of the church and in eternity to come.

And yet, there is still a hunger for it within the one whose mind is attuned to Christ's kingdom, a present-tense thirst for the experience of righteousness in the here-and-now. Can we satisfy that desire in the midst of a world living by different values? Having the desire for righteousness is half the battle, for even among Christians there are too many who are satisfied with what the world offers. But the appeal of God in Isaiah is pointed - "Why do you spend your money for that which is not bread, and your labor for that which does not satisfy?" (3). If the currency is our time, our attention, our love, what do we spend it on? God is offering to let us "buy wine and milk without money and without price" (4), are we taking Him up on it or are we spending ourselves fruitlessly on the emptiness of the world?

Further on in Christ's sermon, He spells this out for His audience: "'Therefore do not be anxious, saying, 'What shall we eat?' or 'What shall we drink?' or 'What shall we wear?' For the Gentiles seek after all these things, and your heavenly Father knows that you need them all. But seek first the kingdom of God and his righteousness, and all these things will be added to you'" (5). If we have in front of us at all times the needs of the kingdom, and our role within it; if we put our spiritual needs before our physical needs then we can trust that God will bring everything else into place too. That is faith, which in itself is a form of righteousness (6) and which allows you to "eat what is good and delight yourselves in rich food" (7)

Bible quotations from the ESV: (1) Rom.14:17 (2) 2 Cor.5:21 (3) Is.55:2 (4) Is.55:1 (5) Matt.6:31-33 (6) Rom.4:3 (7) Is.55:2

CHAPTER FIVE: BLESSED ARE THOSE WHO ARE MERCIFUL (CRAIG JONES)

"Blessed are the merciful, for they shall obtain mercy" (Matt.5:7) There is a story told of the famous French emperor and military general, Napoleon Bonaparte. Several officers and accomplices were discovered in a plot against him and were subsequently sentenced to death for treason. One of them, General Lajolais, had a 14-year-old daughter who, on hearing of the sentence, managed to find a way to appear before Napoleon himself. She threw herself at his feet, crying almost uncontrollably and said, "Sire, mercy for my father, please!" After hearing who her father was, Napoleon replied, "This is the second time he has been found guilty of an attack against the state. He does not deserve mercy." The girl answered, "Sire, it would not be mercy if he deserved it. I plead for mercy!"

This is a good illustration of what 'mercy' really means – the expression of compassion towards someone guilty of an offence, in such a way as to remove the punishment usually required. Simply put, it's the offender not getting what he deserves! When we think about mercy in the context of the Beatitudes of Matthew 5 and their wide scope of applicability amongst all people (1), it's clear that the aspect of 'compassion' included in biblical mercy is what the Lord is drawing attention to as being an admirable characteristic. On a simple level, in situations that can arise in everyday life, it might be seen in giving someone the benefit of the doubt. Perhaps you might hear something negative about someone you know, which seems inconsistent with their character – giving them the benefit of the doubt and not thinking the worst of them would be showing mercy, compassion.

You might have reason to doubt the motivation behind another person's actions towards you or someone else – giving them the benefit of the doubt would be the merciful and compassionate thing to do. Unfortunately, we have a human tendency to want to believe the worst about people, to jump to negative conclusions about them, or the circumstances of the situation they may find themselves in or the motivations for the way they behave. Being merciful means we think more positively about other people.

Of course, it also applies in situations where we have been sinned against, where we have been hurt by someone else physically or emotionally. Instead of retaining bitterness and anger towards the person, we should show a merciful attitude toward them, which, hopefully (if it's not already evident), will bring about a feeling of true sorrow and regret on their part. If they have committed criminal offences, they may continue to face whatever penalty the law imposes, but that does not prevent us granting personal forgiveness, moved by compassion.

This 'beautiful attitude' of mercy is expressed in several different ways in the Bible, which affect the way we should be in our attitude towards other people. For example, it can be seen in the encouragement to "be at peace with all men" (2); to have an attitude that doesn't stir up contention and bad feeling, that doesn't reciprocate any bad feeling expressed towards us. The Lord also said, "In everything, therefore, treat people the same way you want them to treat you" (3). Paul expressed it like this: "So, as those who have been chosen of God, holy and beloved, put on a heart of compassion, kindness, humility, gentleness and patience; bearing with one another and forgiving each other" (4).

And that brings to us a vital perspective that, as those chosen of God, we need to keep in mind as we try to embrace and express this 'beautiful attitude'. We need to constantly remember that we ourselves are the beneficiaries of the greatest expression of mercy that there has ever been, or ever will be. As sinners before a holy and righteous God, we had no defence, no plea, no excuse and, of ourselves, no way to avoid the deserved punishment (5). But in a loving demonstration of extravagant mercy, God diverted our punishment to His Son, Jesus Christ, when He died on the cross at Calvary. When we came to understand that, appreciate it and believe it by faith in our hearts, we received the mercy of God.

As the Lord Himself has said, "I gave you an example that you also should do as I did to you" (6). One of the best ways we can show mercy to others is by sharing with them the life-changing message that we ourselves have believed, that they too may come to believe in the Lord Jesus and receive God's mercy.

Bible quotations from the NASB: (1) see Matt.7:28 (2) Rom.12:18 (3) Matt.7:12 (4) Col.3:12-13 (5) Rom.6:23 (6) Jn.13:15

CHAPTER SIX: BLESSED ARE THOSE WHO ARE PURE IN HEART (ANDREW DORRICOTT)

How can we see God when the Bible is clear that no one has seen God at any time (1)? The Bible is also clear about our sinful nature (2), so how is it possible for us to be pure? While purity speaks of being clean, it is also a word meaning 'free from extraneous matter; simple or homogenous'. God knows our heart. In the days of Noah, God saw that people's hearts were continually evil (3). David cried out to the Lord, in the grieving of his sin, for God to purify his heart (4). And in John's Gospel it says that Jesus knew the hearts of everyone (5). It is at the centre of His plan to change our hearts and to cleanse them from all unrighteousness. Our heart speaks of the innermost driving force of what we do and say (6), and God is ultimately concerned with the condition of it – not only to the point of salvation, however.

Many Christians, and many non-Christians too, for that matter, want to see God at work; perhaps in the midst of a trial, or when facing a big decision, or when praying on someone's behalf. It can be the case where we feel or see very little from God, and that can be a stumbling block in our faith journey. The issues of life are not always an "all's well that ends well" experience, and the perceived lack of action by God can be difficult to understand and accept. When we seek God's help, or His direction, are we single-minded in our heart towards God, or do we feel as though praying to God is just one of many steps to get the answer? Are we so distracted by other situations, people or 'idols' around us that we are unable to see God at work?

Using a specific trial or decision might not be enough to explain this verse, so let's take the principle of a pure heart in the face of an issue and expand it to our daily lives. In a self-assessment of the things you hold dear in your life, can you say that your heart is 'free from extraneous matter' in your devotion and commitment to God? This really is the heart of the verse: to live a life free from idols (meaning anything that distracts our devotion away from God). It is a very hard thing to achieve, but perhaps more troubling is that it's very easy to justify not doing so. For fear of reaction or offence, we can compartmentalise our lives into family, work/school, friends, and ourselves as individuals. We can be slightly different people in these different environments, adapting to the social norms or conventions so that we fit in, or succeed, by the world's definition. We justify it by calling it 'balance'. This seems contrary to Romans 12 (7).

If we are able to live our life with a heart that is single-minded, free from extraneous matter, pure in devotion to God, we will see Him more and more at work in our lives and the lives of those around us. We will be more in tune with His Word and His will. Not only will we better see His direction when we ask, but we will see His direction even before we ask. Seeing God in our lives is as much about seeing and recognising the effect of God in all situations, big and small, as it is seeing Him face to face in that future day. Being pure in heart is not strictly a matter of being clean, but being undivided in our devotion in the depth of our heart toward God. A truly undivided heart will establish, maintain and grow our relationship with God to unknown heights. Set aside all the reasoning and justification for those things that distract you from God and conform you to the world, and God will be visible in mighty ways!

Bible quotations from the NASB: (1) Ex.33:20; Jn.1:18; 6:46; 1 Jn.4:12 (2) Rom.3:23; 1 Jn.1:8 (3) Gen.6:5 (4) Ps.51:10 (5) Jn.2:24, also Matt.9:4 (6) Matt.12:34 (7) Rom.12:2

CHAPTER SEVEN: BLESSED ARE THE PEACEMAKERS (ANDY SEDDON)

"Blessed are the peacemakers, for they shall be called sons of God" (Matt.5:9). Is it true that much TV entertainment takes advantage of people not getting on with each other? It could be a reality show or a talent contest. Some of it might be healthy competition, but often it is the arguments and fights which have the public talking afterwards. I suppose these shows would be a little boring if all the characters got on well and were nice to each other! In total contrast to this, Jesus declares: "Blessed are the peacemakers" (1). These are people who actively promote harmony and reconciliation.

The New Testament word, 'reconciliation' simply means 'to change'. This would be evident, for example, when enemies change into friends or when anger changes into forgiveness. Jesus goes on to say that peacemakers shall be called "sons of God". Why? It is because children take after their parents, and our heavenly Father is the ultimate peacemaker. There are three things that the Bible shows us to be true about God the peacemaker, and therefore should be true also of those claiming to be His children.

God Loves Reconciliation

Making peace with sinful, rebellious human beings has been at the centre of God's plan ever since Adam and Eve first became His enemies. A wise woman once said to King David: "God will not take away life, and he devises means so that the banished one will not remain an outcast" (2). Reconciliation and restoration are themes at the centre of God's heart. If we have personal faith in Jesus Christ, then we have already experienced for ourselves the peace that God brings. In the words of Paul: "you who once were far off have been brought near by the blood of Christ" (3). If we enjoy this divine peace, then we too should be active in promoting peace with others, especially with our spiritual family who share our salvation. To tolerate bickering and conflict without taking action is not an option. We are to "seek peace and pursue it" (4). We are to be "eager to maintain the unity of the Spirit" (5). We are to "strive for peace with everyone" (6). These words imply earnest, positive action: 'seek', 'pursue', 'maintain', 'strive'.

God Acted First

Reconciliation was God's plan, not ours. This is amazing when we remember that God was the innocent and injured party! The Bible states: "all this is from God" (7). It was "while we were still sinners, Christ died for us" (8). If you are like me, then you may be prone to stubbornness! If, in the middle of a conflict with somebody, I think – and I stress the word 'think!' – I'm in the right, then I am less likely to take peace-making steps, because this would inflict a painful blow to my pride! After all, why can't the other person come to me? Well, if I am a true child of God, would I not take the initiative, just as God took the initiative for me?

Disunity harms our spiritual service for God. Jesus commands: "So if you are offering your gift at the altar and there remember that your brother has something against you ... First be reconciled to your brother, and then come and offer your gift" (9). Notice here how I must take the step when I am aware my brother has a problem with me!

God Made a Phenomenal Sacrifice

When we've been hurt, taking steps to be reconciled might feel costly. It may cost time or energy, it may require a change in our attitude and behaviour, and it may even feel humiliating! Consider carefully however the price that God has paid: "while we were enemies we were reconciled to God by the death of his Son" (10). God's love knows no limits. He gave what was most precious to Him so that we could know divine peace. As we think about this, let us pray for the help of the Holy Spirit to bear "with one another ... forgiving each other; as the Lord has forgiven you ..." (11).

Only when we practise these 'upside down' teachings of the Lord will we know the happiness of being free children of God.

Bible quotations from the ESV: (1) Matt.5:9 (2) 2 Sam.14:14 (3) Eph.2:13 (4) 1 Pet.3:11 (5) Eph.4:3 (6) Heb.12:14 (7) 2 Cor.5:18 (8) Rom.5:8 (9) Matt.5:23-24 (10) Rom.5:10 (11) Col.3:13

CHAPTER EIGHT: BLESSED ARE THOSE WHO ARE PERSECUTED (RICHARD HUTCHINSON)

"Blessed are those who are persecuted for righteousness' sake, for theirs is the kingdom of heaven. Blessed are you when others revile you and persecute you and utter all kinds of evil against you falsely on my account. Rejoice and be glad, for your reward is great in heaven, for so they persecuted the prophets who were before you" (1).

The last of the Beatitudes is for those who are persecuted. It is not a subject that I have much personal experience of, and while I am tempted to insert a sincere "Praise the Lord" in there, I wonder whether that lack of persecution is not a comment on the stand I take for the faith. After all, the Scriptures make it very clear in the New Testament that suffering and persecution were to be expected in the Christian life. Indeed, all who desire to live a godly life in Christ Jesus will be persecuted, Paul told Timothy (2), and Peter was just as matter-of-fact in his first epistle: "Beloved, do not be surprised at the fiery trial when it comes upon you to test you, as though something strange were happening to you. But rejoice insofar as you share Christ's sufferings, that you may also rejoice and be glad when his glory is revealed" (3).

So if I find myself in the position of a comfortable Christian, should I rejoice, or should I be asking myself whether my life is not Godly enough to warrant the persecution which is an inevitable consequence for Paul? Should I be surprised at the lack of fiery trials, since that seemed the stranger thing to Peter; concerned that I am not sharing in Christ's sufferings to the degree I should be?

The New Testament writers prepared the saints for difficulties as the natural course of things and in doing so they were following on from the teaching of the Lord Jesus. Not only was the Lord alluding to the suffering to be endured on His account in the Beatitudes, but He was repeatedly explicit in flagging up the reality of following Him. In John 15:11, after a glorious description of the close relationship with God available through Him as the true vine, which Jesus said He was describing "that My joy may be in you and your joy may be full", He outlines clearly that aligning ourselves with God and abiding in Him would mean separating ourselves from the world, which the world would hate us for, just as it hated the Lord Jesus: "If they persecuted Me they will also persecute you" (4).

The very qualification Jesus gives for anyone willing to follow after Him is: "Let him deny himself and take up his cross daily ..." (5). He wasn't hiding the fact that following after Him would bring sacrifice and suffering along with it. The promise of the Lord for those who suffer for His sake is that "theirs is the kingdom of heaven" and "your reward is great in heaven". Persecution is called 'a fiery trial' by Peter, and it is the purpose of any test or trial to prove the value of something. The testing of our faith in persecution reaps its rewards. "We rejoice in our sufferings, knowing that suffering produces endurance, and endurance produces character, and character produces hope" (6). That hope is the hope of glory; the joy of knowing that this world is only a temporary dwelling for us, and "So we do not lose heart ... For this light momentary affliction is preparing for us an eternal weight of glory beyond all comparison" (7).

With such a rich blessing comes the challenge. When the apostles were arrested and beaten for their preaching we read they went "rejoicing that they were counted worthy to suffer dishonour for the name" (8). If persecution comes to those who live Godly lives and if I have not been afflicted, what is missing from my life to be counted worthy of sharing in the sufferings of my Lord and Saviour? If we are found worthy to endure trials, the challenge then is to "Count it all joy" (9), to "joyfully accept" (10) whatever shape affliction takes and to be content with (11) the hardships of following the one who endured the cross for us for the joy set before Him. He has set before us a joy that should encourage us through whatever this passing world can throw at us.

Bible quotations from the ESV: (1) Matt.5:10-12 (2) 2 Tim.3:12 (3) 1 Pet.4:12-13 (4) Jn.15:20 (5) Lk.9:23 (6) Rom.5:3-4 (7) 2 Cor.4:16-18 (8) Acts 5:41 (9) Jas.1:2 (10) Heb.10:34 (11) 2 Cor.12:10

Did you love *Collected Writings On ... The Cross of Christ*?
Then you should read *Bible Covenants 101* by Hayes Press!

The topic of "Bible Covenants" might seem to be an unusual subject, but it's vitally important to get to grips with to understand how God wants to have a relationship with mankind. This little guide is a perfect way to get a quick introduction to the subject. The first chapter reviewing the main components of the Biblical covenant with the following chapters taking a look at the main covenants in the Bible, as well as some lesser well-known ones. The final chapters analyse the progression of these covenants from Old to New Testament, from the Old Covenant to the New Covenant, and the final chapter concludes the book with a look at the relevance of the use of the word "Testament".

Why do we have Old and New Testaments and how is this related to covenants?

About the Publisher

Hayes Press (www.hayespress.org) is a registered charity in the United Kingdom, whose primary mission is to disseminate the Word of God, mainly through literature. It is one of the largest distributors of gospel tracts and leaflets in the United Kingdom, with over 100 titles and hundreds of thousands despatched annually.

Hayes Press also publishes Plus Eagles Wings, a fun and educational Bible magazine for children, six times a year and Golden Bells, a popular daily Bible reading calendar in wall or desk formats.

Also available are over 100 Bibles in many different versions, shapes and sizes, Christmas cards, Christian jewellery, Eikos Bible Art, Bible text posters and much more!

Printed in Great Britain
by Amazon